The lending of Bodleian printed books and manuscripts

HENRY WILLIAM CHANDLER

Remarks on the practice and policy of lending
Bodleian printed books and manuscripts

TABLE OF CONTENTS

PREFACE

The present 'Remarks' are a reprint, with many omissions and additions, of two privately printed papers which were communicated to the Curators last year. From November, 1884, for about twelve months, I did very little more than watch attentively the way in which Bodleian business is transacted, to me at once a novelty and a surprise. For some purposes writing is preferable to talking, and accordingly in November, 1885, I printed a memorandum containing many gentle hints—φωνᾶντα συνετοῖσιν—which I faintly hoped might eventually prove beneficial to the Library. Next came a Memorandum 'on the Classed Catalogue,' a thing which some Curators look on as a most valuable work, and others as an interminable and wasteful absurdity. This was followed by a paper 'on the Bodleian Coins and Medals', with some observations on the proposal to transfer the collection to the Ashmolean Museum. As far as could be seen, all this expenditure of ink and money did no harm, and no good. In May, 1886, a committee was appointed to draw up regulations for loans of books; and in June the Curators received a paper 'on the lending of Bodleian Books and Manuscripts,' as also Bishop Barlow's Argument against lending them, then for the first time printed as a whole; and in both the illegality of the borrowers' list was pointed out, and very broad hints given, not only that the present loan statute is defective, but why, and in what manner it is so. If these hints, facts, and arguments had been addressed to the twelve signs of the Zodiac, they could not have produced less visible effect; and it was wonderfully amusing to find, that more than half my brethren could not for the life of them see what to everybody else was plain as a pikestaff; so on we went in the well-beaten path, steady as old Time himself, looking neither to the right hand nor to the left, and, what is more remarkable, never for one moment looking ahead. Finally, at the beginning of October, came a paper on 'Book-lending as practised at the Bodleian'; and this proved to be the last straw; for on October 30th, partly by words and partly by that silence which gives consent, it was plainly intimated that these papers were unwelcome. One friend, and only one, had a good word to say for them; so far as they contained collection of facts he approved of them, but no further. As my little experiment failed so lamentably, I am hardly likely to repeat it, or to put so severe a strain on the good nature and patience of my colleagues as ever again to trouble them with a scrap of printed paper. This puts me into a sort of quandary. I abhor pen and ink, and should like to hold my tongue and spare my pocket; but that is impossible as things are. I cannot stand by and see men who know no better trying (with the best possible intentions) to get the Bodleian on to an inclined plane, down which it must rapidly slide to perdition, without loudly protesting against their acts. What then is to be done? Private feelings must be respected, yet not so as to impede the performance of a duty to the Library and to the University. The atmosphere of a meeting is not conducive to calm and rational discussion; I cannot make speeches; the board does not relish either facts or arguments in print. Only one course remains then; whenever there is anything to be said about the Bodleian or its management (and there is much that ought to be, and must be said sooner or later), it shall no longer be privately printed and given away to unwilling recipients, but published and sold. In this way all parties will be satisfied: those who are interested in the Library can buy; those who are not, can protect themselves against annoyance. So much by way of explanation.

When at length the board determined to apply for a new statute, and did in November what anybody but ourselves would have done in June, the hope was expressed that the statute would be introduced at once, and then pushed through Congregation and Convocation as rapidly as possible in the present term; whereupon somebody observed, that it would be just as well not to hurry the business; and this seems to have been the view adopted by Council.

If Convocation could only seize the full significance and incalculable value to present and future generations of a library of reference, a library, that is, where, at all lawful times, every book deposited in it should always be forthcoming in a moment, it would at once see that from such a library no lending whatever ought to be permitted, simply because lending and deposit are practical contradictories; and if Convocation could plainly see this, it would make very short work of any statute which legalized loans. There is no denying, however, that in the present day the public mind, as it is playfully called, and the University mind as well, is in a wonderfully flabby condition. Nobody seems to be thoroughly convinced of the unquestionable truth, that every possible plan in this world is open to objections more or less serious, and so they go hunting about for a scheme that shall embrace all good and exclude all evil; such people are emphatically limp and unpractical. All that is offered to our choice here below is a lesser evil, and experience has proved over and over again, that it is a lesser evil never to lend a book out of such a library as the Bodleian, than it is to lend one. But if the University in its inscrutable wisdom should choose to do the wrong thing, there are more ways than one of doing it,—

ἐσθλοὶ μὲν γὰρ ἁπλῶς, παντοδαπῶς δὲ κακοί.

It might, for instance, confine the actual granting of a loan to Convocation. If an application for a book were made, the University might impose on the Curators the duty of stating in writing their reasons for advocating the loan, and Convocation might determine to lend, if it judged those reasons to be sound. This would be an approximation to what was the law (though not by any means the practice) prior to 1873; nor could it be described as a retrograde step, unless the reformation of a bad habit is necessarily a step backwards.

If, however, the University resolves to copy the practice of foreign libraries, it might be wise, first, to appoint a small committee to discover and report what that practice really is. If, like a mob of monkeys, we are determined to imitate, it is just as well that our imitation should be a good one, and not a caricature.

In either, or indeed in any, case some effectual provision should be made for enforcing the statute; it ought no longer to be possible for the Curators to act with impunity as they have been in the habit of acting for almost a quarter of a century.

A good many of my friends are strong party men of a more or less rabid type, and I hope that they are well informed when they tell me that this purely literary question about the Bodleian is not going to be turned into one of those faction fights, which occasionally disturb and disgrace this place; but that each man will judge for himself, and vote accordingly, without divesting himself of what little reason he may happen to possess, and blindly following a leader, who may know and care less about the matter than he does himself. I hope that it will be so, yet I have my doubts; for this vile spirit of faction clings like the robe of Nessus to all who have ever been weak enough, or wicked enough, to yield to its temptations; and one side is just as bad as the other. Whether Convocation can be got to see the real question in these unlearned and vulgar times may be questionable; at any rate, I should have felt myself a traitor to Bodley, to Oxford, and to learning itself, if I had not done what little I could to prevent an act, which, if perpetrated, must end, sooner or later, in the irreparable damage, or the complete destruction of a library intended by its founder to be a perpetual help to all true scholars, an inexhaustible treasure-house of learning to last as long as England itself.

H. W. C.

Oxford,

Jan. 15th, 1887.

REMARKS ON THE PRACTICE AND POLICY OF LENDING BODLEIAN PRINTED BOOKS AND MANUSCRIPTS

Before offering any remarks on the policy of lending books out of the Bodleian Library it may be well to give a brief account of the practice of lending, so far as it has been sanctioned there. From the foundation of the Library down to 1873, though practised, it cannot be said to have been sanctioned at all, except as regards certain books given on the condition that they should be lent.

On the 20th of June, 1610, a complete Bodleian Statute was promulgated and confirmed in Convocation (Appendix Statutorum, p. 5 sqq. ed. 1763). This statute was drawn up by Sir Thomas Bodley himself, and the eighth section of it—'de Libris extra Bibliothecam non ferendis, aut ullo modo commodandis'—fully expresses his firm and rooted detestation of book-lending. Bodley's own words, of which the Latin statute is a literal translation, run thus:—

"And sith the sundry Examples of former Ages, as well in this University, as in other Places of the Realm, have taught us over-often, that the frequent Loan of Books, hath bin a principal occasion of the Ruin and Destruction of many famous Libraries; It is therefore ordered and decreed to be observed as a Statute of irrevocable Force, that for no Regard, Pretence, or Cause, there shall at any time, any Volume, either of these that are chained, or of others unchained, be given or lent, to any Person or Persons, of whatsoever State or Calling, upon any kind of Caution, or offer of Security, for his faithful Restitution; and that no such Book or Volume shall at any time, by any whatsoever, be carried forth of the Library, for any longer space, or other uses, and Purposes, than if need so require, to be sold away for altogether, as being superfluous or unprofitable; or changed for some other of a better Edition; or being over-worn to be new bound again, and immediately returned, from whence it was removed. For the Execution whereof in every Particular, there shall no Man intermeddle, but the Keeper himself alone, who is also to proceed with the Knowledge, Liking, and Direction of those Publick Overseers, whose Authority we will notify in other Statutes ensuing[1]."

[1] Reliquiæ Bodleianæ, p. 27.

This statute has the great merit of being so plain and clear, that no one could mistake its meaning. It was further fenced about by the statute 'de materia indispensabili,' Tit. X.§11.5, as explained in 'Barlow's Argument,' p. 6. It was not totally and absolutely impossible to borrow a book from the Bodleian, but it was only Convocation, moved to the act in a solemn and specified way, that could by any legal means lend it. From 1610 to 1856, then, such was the law which everybody in the University was bound to obey, and, as far as I can discover, everybody did obey it, with the few exceptions that will presently be mentioned.

In 1624 William, Bishop of Lincoln, wished to borrow a book, but was denied[2]. In 1628 Sir Thomas Roe gave twenty-nine manuscripts, and "proposed that his books should be permitted to be lent out for purposes of printing, on proper security being given; a proposition which was accepted by Convocation[3]." In 1629 the Earl of Pembroke presented the Barocci Collection, and "he was willing that the MSS. should, if necessary, be allowed to be borrowed." Borrowed accordingly they were, and one at least suffered irreparable injury in very early days[4]. In 1634 we were presented with Sir Kenelm Digby's splendid manuscripts: "the donor stipulated that they should not be strictly confined to use within the walls of the Library;" but afterwards left the University to treat them as it pleased[5]; so that they fell under the general Bodleian Statute.

[2] Barlow's Argument, p. 9.
[3] Macray, Annals, p. 51.
[4] Barlow, p. 10; Macray, Annals, p. 55.
[5] Macray, Annals, p. 59.

Between 1635 and 1640 came Laud's magnificent donations. He "directs in his letter of gift, that none of the books shall on any account be taken out of the Library 'nisi solum ut typis mandentur, et sic publici et juris et utilitatis fiant,' upon sufficient security, to be approved by the Vice-Chancellor and Proctors; the MS. in such cases being immediately after printing restored to its place in the Library[6]." This stipulation of Laud should be carefully borne in mind, because it will be found that of late years the Curators have not observed the terms of the gift. Doubtless they did not know what Laud's directions were; yet men who undertake the office of trustees are bound to know their duties. In 1636 the University refused leave to Laud himself, who wished to borrow Rob. Hare's MS. Liber

Privilegiorum Universitatis[7]. In 1645 Charles I, in ignorance of our statutes, applied for a book and was refused; in 1654 Cromwell wanted a book for the Portuguese Ambassador, and was likewise refused[8]; and it is much to the credit of both, that they not only acquiesced, but expressed their approval of the Bodleian rule.

[6] Macray, Annals, p. 61.

[7] Macray, Annals, p. 82.

[8] Barlow's Argument, p. 9.

On August 29, 1654, a grace was passed in Convocation, which permitted Selden to borrow MSS. from the collections of Barocci, Roe, and Digby, provided he did not have more than three at a time, and that he gave bond in £100 (not £1000 as Hearne states[9]) for the return of each of them within a year[10]. Barlow[11] declares that this was illegal and null; and it may be observed in passing that the whole history of the Selden bequest needs fresh investigation. This same year that grand scholar's books began to arrive in Oxford, and his executors stipulated, as a condition of the gift, that no book from his collection should hereafter be lent to any person upon any condition whatsoever. This also must by no means be forgotten, because we shall by and by see the Curators again and again strangely oblivious of the conditions on which the University received these invaluable books.

[9] Barlow's Argument, p. 3.

[10] Macray, Annals, p. 79.

[11] Argument, p. 8.

At the Visitation on Nov. 8, 1686, it was ordered that notice be given that 'nullus in posterum quemlibet librum aut volumen extra Bibliothecam asportet,' and that monition be sent to every College and Hall for the return of any books taken out within three days[12].

[12] Macray, Annals, p. 109.

In 1789 a lazy and incompetent Librarian, John Price, is said to have lent the Rector of Lincoln a copy of Cook's Voyages, presented to the Library by George III, telling him that the longer he kept it the better, 'for if it was known to be in the Library, he (Price) should be perpetually plagued with enquiries after it[13].' What the Curators were about to permit such irregularities it is difficult to imagine; at any rate here you had eight picked men—Dr. Joseph Chapman, President of Trinity, Vice-Chancellor; the two Proctors; Dr. Randolph, Professor of Divinity, and afterwards successively Bishop of Oxford and of Bangor; Dr. Vansittart, Professor of Civil Law; Dr. Vivian, Professor of Medicine; Dr. Blayney, Professor of Hebrew; William Jackson, Professor of Greek and afterwards Bishop of Oxford:— they are men, citizens, members of a learned corporation, trustees; they have solemnly sworn by everything which they profess to hold sacred, that they will faithfully observe the statutes; and what was required of them? As much sense of duty as you expect and commonly find in a watcher or a gamekeeper; yet, till they were roused by the public protest of Dr. Beddowes, they seem to have shewed no trace or feeling of responsibility at all.

[13] Macray, Annals, p. 198.

Down to the year 1856 the Bodleian Curators were eight in number, namely, the Vice-Chancellor, the two Proctors, and the Regius Professors of Divinity, Hebrew, Greek, Medicine, and Civil Law. Eight is rather a large number, and the larger any board is the weaker becomes the sense of personal responsibility. No man feels that he is answerable for anything, because he is sunk and extinguished in a majority or a minority; and yet, without a keen sense of personal responsibility, all business is laxly and badly done, even when it is done at all. The artificial privacy of our proceedings is also an evil. In theory all our meetings are public, so far at least as Convocation is concerned; in fact, they are private; yet, if the University always knew not only what is done, but who it is that does it; if our acts were duly published, as they ought to be, in the University Gazette, probably both board and University would be the better for it, and it is certain that the affairs of the Library would be none the worse.

If Bodley argued that men who teach a subject are necessarily acquainted with its literature, and are consequently the fittest guardians and directors of a library, he argued very badly, and in ignorance of facts. Ability to teach a subject is one thing; knowledge of the literature of that subject—such knowledge as is required in the superintendents of a library—is a totally different thing. The two may be indeed united, but very rarely are so. A man, for instance, may be a finished Latin scholar without ever having heard of Coster's Donatus, and without being able to offer an opinion on that or on any of the other editions in which Dutch libraries glory. Probably not one man in fifty who reads the sentence which I have just written will have the very remotest idea of its true meaning; and if he has not, it will not follow that he is a dunce, or that he is a poor Latinist; all that follows is that he has much to learn before he is fit to take any part in the management of a large library. What is wanted, what in fact is necessary, is that sort of knowledge which the Italian government proposes to give to all employed in the libraries under its control. In Rome and in Florence a course of bibliographical instruction and examination has lately been instituted. The syllabus of the course, which is a very good one, lies before me, and in it the subject is divided into six parts: 1. Paleografia, 2. Bibliologia, 3. Bibliografia, 4. Biblioteconomia, 5. Amministrazione, 6. Lingue. The knowledge required is neither recondite nor profound, yet I shudder to think what the result would be were we Curators to submit ourselves to the tender mercies of this Italian board. To speak for myself, I should have faced such an examination without the least trepidation some twenty years ago; but now, though I have been trying to brush up faded knowledge, I would not stake a single sixpence on a favorable issue; and to judge from all I have seen and heard during the last two years, I suspect that, though a few might perhaps scramble through, the great majority of us would emerge from the ordeal more completely plucked than was the unhappy bird, which Diogenes introduced to the astonished disciples with the words 'Here is Plato's man!'

In 1856 the University, probably suspecting that the board as originally constituted was not the best that could be devised, yet timidly shrinking from a radical and salutary reform, endeavoured to improve matters by a measure which, if it remedied one defect, unquestionably increased another. It made a board already too large, still larger by the addition of five members elected by Congregation. In the course of thirty years fourteen different men have been so elected. That all were properly qualified to discharge the duties of their office no one will assert who knows what those qualifications are. Why they were chosen the University best knows. If Congregation would but remember what a unique and priceless treasure it possesses in this noble library, if it only knew how easy it is for rashness and ignorance to damage and to ruin it, how difficult it is even for knowledge to preserve it, ability and willingness to serve it would be the indispensable and the only qualifications demanded, and neither age nor rank, dignity, nor above all party, would be for one moment taken into account. It may be remarked that all the thirteen Curators very rarely attend a meeting: in the course of the last two years such a thing has happened once only; but a board, the members of which attend intermittently, is apt to show signs of discontinuity in its proceedings; and a firm, consistent policy is as necessary in the management of a library as it is in any other affair of life. What is wanted in Curators is common sense, business capacity, and a special knowledge of books. No one would dream of appointing any man an inspector of locomotives on a railway, unless he were thoroughly acquainted with the structure and working of a locomotive, and capable, at a push, of driving it himself: a large library is as complex as a locomotive, and quite as difficult to manage effectively. Experts, who are not so numerous as might be supposed, will back me in this assertion; but Convocation must not be astonished if it is hotly and contemptuously denied.

The minutes of the Curators' Meetings begin on March 20, 1793, and, with a break of some four years when there are none (from Nov. 26, 1849, to May 27, 1854), they continue to the present time.

On Dec. 7, 1803, four printed books were allowed to go out of the Library 'for the use of the Clarendon Press, to be returned when done with,' contrary to statute so far as appears; and there was a somewhat similar transaction on June 2, 1815.

On Nov. 27, 1841, the sum of £500 was paid for the Sanscrit MSS. of Prof.

H. H. Wilson, who 'stipulated that the Boden Professor of Sanscrit for the time being should be allowed the privilege of borrowing MSS. (not more than two volumes at one time), giving for them a receipt, and engagement for their safe return.'

In 1850 came the Government Commission. The Commissioners have a good deal to say about the Bodleian, which will be found in their Report made in 1852, p. 115 sqq. I do not quote their remarks for a reason which appears to me valid. There were seven Commissioners all told, and although they were very eminent persons, there was not one amongst them, so far as I can discover, who had any special knowledge of libraries, or of the best way of managing them. Moreover, I myself heard one of those seven Commissioners say, more than once in the course of conversation, that he should think it no particular misfortune if the Bodleian and its contents were totally destroyed. Nor do I feel called upon to incur the expense of reproducing in extenso the evidence on which the Commissioners based their recommendations. It may be sufficient to say that the following witnesses were in favour of the lending system, some with restrictions and some with hardly any:—the Rev. R. W. Browne; the Rev. R. Walker; the Rev. B. Jowett; the Rev. W. H. Cox; E. A. Freeman, Esq.; the Rev. H. Wall; the Rev. R. Congreve; Sir E. Head; N. S. Maskelyne, Esq.; and the Rev. J. Griffiths. It is not very easy to say whether Prof. H. H. Wilson and Dr. Greenhill did or did not belong to the lending party; but if they did, they proposed such restrictions as would materially lessen the evil. Prof. H. H. Vaughan (a most wordy person) wished to confine the right of borrowing to the Professors. Against lending were H. E. Strickland, Esq.; Prof. W. F. Donkin; the Rev. R. Scott; Travers Twiss, Esq.; Dr. Macbride; the Rev. E. S. Ffoulkes; and Dr. Phillimore: and I hope nobody will be offended if I say that knowledge of books and the way to use them is, as might be expected, very much more conspicuous in those who oppose lending than in those who advocate it. The Rev. R. W. Browne observes, that 'probably manuscripts and such books as are unable to be replaced should not be lent, because it would be quite worth the while of those who wished to consult them to visit the Library for that purpose.' It is not often that one meets with so cogent a piece of reasoning, and Mr. Browne's 'because' proves that he had studied Logic with considerable benefit; he also thinks that the system in the Public Library at Cambridge 'works well.' Another witness tells us that 'the experience of the Cambridge University Library, and of many foreign libraries, shews that this [i. e. lending under certain restrictions] can be done without danger, and with small loss compared to the immense benefit obtained by it.' Sir Edmund Head also admires the Göttingen and Cambridge plan, and avers that experience has proved that the risk of loss and damage is groundless. How different are these airy speculations from the hard facts of Mr. Bradshaw the Cambridge

Librarian, of the Librarian of the Advocates' Library at Edinburgh, and of Mr. Panizzi (see below, p. 50 sqq.); but then these gentlemen had the immense and perhaps unfair advantage of knowing what they were talking about.

In 1853 a Report and Evidence upon the recommendations of H. M.'s Commissioners was presented to the Heads of Houses. "The Committee think that the opportunity at present allowed for lending books in special cases, by permission of Convocation, is sufficient to meet extreme cases; and that it is unnecessary to give power to the Curators to lend books from the Library."

Dr. Pusey's evidence (p. 172) is that of a man who knows something of books, and he points out how very fallacious is Sir E. Head's reference to the Göttingen Library, which is altogether of a different character from the Bodleian. "In 1825 it consisted almost entirely of modern books, and whatever accessions it may since have had, it cannot, like the Bodleian, have any large proportion of books, which, if lost, could not be replaced." Dr. Pusey is strongly against lending Bodleian books; but how little of principle there was in his objection will be seen further on, where we shall find him more than once advocating loans. The Rev. C. Marriott is also, on very sensible grounds, against lending; yet it should in common fairness be known that he borrowed a most valuable manuscript out of Oriel College Library, and died with it in his possession. It was nearly sent to Africa by his executors, and was at last, together with other books, actually given (in all innocence of course) to Bradfield College, from which establishment Oriel at last retrieved it; so that in his case, as in that of Dr. Pusey, excellent principles were joined to very loose practice.

Dr. Bandinel, Bodley's Librarian, gives evidence which is short and sweet. "However weighty some reasons may appear, the evidence materially preponderates against lending books out of the Library. I need only quote one great authority, that of Niebuhr," which he does; the passage is given below, p. 49. Dr. Bandinel also adds, "I have had a long conversation with the Librarian of the Advocates' Library at Edinburgh, who stated, that upon comparing the books in that Library with their different Catalogues previous to the formation of a new Catalogue, it was found that owing to the practice of lending books from the Library they had lost upwards of 6000, indeed very near 7000 works." Evidence, p. 325; an instructive comment on the lending system.

About this time, however, 'University Reform,' the true meaning of which most of us here know, was in the air, and on May 22, 1856, the old Library Statutes were abolished and an entirely new one enacted. Bodley's own statute against letting books go out of the Library was of course abrogated. That Convocation still retained the right to lend is beyond question; but did anybody else, Curators or Librarian, acquire the right to do so? That the

University did not intend to convey any such right seems perfectly clear; for the 11th clause of the new statute (which is identical with the present statute, Tit. XX. iii. § 11, paragraphs 1 to 6) is headed "De libris extra Bibliothecam ad tempus detinendis, aut etiam efferendis." Now whoever says 'or even to have them taken out,' and then proceeds to order whither they shall be taken, namely to the Camera, forbids by implication their removal from the Library on any other terms, or to any other place than those expressly mentioned. That the University, whatever its intentions may have been, did not as a matter of fact convey the right to any one is obvious from the statute itself; and as the Curators never at any time possessed the right of lending books, it is equally plain that they could not acquire it without an express commission from the University. That the Curators themselves were of this opinion is clear from a resolution of theirs arrived at on Oct. 29, 1859, more than three years after the statute was passed. I should say that in the interval no loan was sanctioned by Convocation, or, so far as appears, even applied for. On Oct. 29, 1859, nine Curators being present, 'The Vice-Chancellor mentioned the desire of the Rev. Mr. —— to be allowed to have books out of the Bodleian Library for the purposes of study by Grace of Convocation. The Curators resolved:—That it was not expedient that such a proposition should be made to Convocation.' The Curators, or a majority of them, did not dream of arrogating to themselves the power of lending, and they, as well as the applicant, assume as self-evident that books could not be borrowed. Books could be sent to the Camera; they could not go elsewhere without the sanction of Convocation. The new statute then did not make lending (except by Convocation) lawful, nor was there any intention to make it lawful.

That same year, on Nov. 8, a Curator gave notice that he would move:—'That Books and MSS. be taken out of the Bodleian Library under special conditions with consent of the Curators;' that is, according to my view of the case, he gave notice of a motion to take by force and illegally a power which the University had not given; but it does not appear by the minutes that any such motion was actually made.

On Oct. 25, 1860, 'leave was granted by Convocation for the lending two Laud Manuscripts, 561 and 563, being copies of the Historia Hierosoylmitana, by Albert of Aix, to the French Government.' Of this loan there is, I believe, no trace in the minutes, but it is one more [14]proof that the Curators, or a majority of them, did not believe either in their right or in their power to lend books. Whether Convocation lent these two Laudian manuscripts under bond duly approved, and for the purposes of publication, Mr. Macray does not state; but it looks very much as if the University was just as ignorant of its obligations as the Curators of a later date were of theirs.

[14] Macray, Annals, p. 295.

On Feb. 4, 1862, a man applied for a printed book, which he wanted for a law case in which he was engaged; the result was this:—"Resolved—That, there being nothing in the present statutes to forbid the exercise of the discretion of the Curators in such a case, the book in question be lent, under such securities and with such precautions as the Librarian may deem necessary." Let any man read the eleventh and twelfth sections of the present Bodleian Statute (identical, so far as the present question is concerned, with that of 1856), and he will see that no discretion is left to the Curators at all; there is no hint, however faint, of "such a case." In 1862, Feb. 4, the Curators assume that they have a power to lend books; on Nov. 7 of the same year they go a step further, for they leave it 'to the discretion of the Librarian to lend, if he shall deem fit, a certain MS. to the Belgian Government.' Having themselves no power to lend, they authorise the Librarian to lend if he chooses.

In 1863, Feb. 17, notice was given of the following motion:—'That on application from the Professors teaching at the Museum the Bodley Librarian be empowered to lend, for a limited time, any books bearing on the subjects there taught that are wanted by the Students at the Museum; the books to be returned at the end of each term:' and on March 17 of the same year this motion was carried with certain alterations, 'and it was resolved that it should be referred to the Council with a view on their approval of obtaining the sanction of Convocation'; in other words, the Curators acknowledged that Convocation could lend, and that they themselves could not lawfully do so.

In 1859 the Curators, or a majority of them, are clear that they have no power to lend: in 1862 they assume that they have the power, moreover they exercise it, and they authorise the Librarian to lend a MS. to the Belgian Government; yet on Feb. 16, 1864, they appear to disclaim this power, for they resolve, 'That it be proposed to Convocation to lend three Icelandic MSS.—to the Icelandic Society in Copenhagen at the request of the Danish Minister.' They either had the power to lend, or they had not: if they had, this application to Convocation was unnecessary; if they had not, they had been occupied for some time in the not very dignified employment of ignoring a statute which it was their peculiar duty to observe.

On April 20, 1864, Dr. Pusey most inconsistently moves that a Syriac MS. be lent; and on May 11 lent it was.

In 1865, March 11, a foreigner has leave 'to borrow Arabian MSS., provided the application for the use thereof be made through the Saxon Minister, and a bond for £50 entered into for the safe return.'

On June 3, 'the use of Manuscripts 169—187 was granted on the application of Lord John Russell to the French Government for the use of the Imprimerie of Parisfor two months.'

In 1866 the Curators lent manuscripts to the University Library of Göttingen; and in 1868, Jan. 31, 'it was resolved to lend MS. Selden B. 31 to the Prussian Government.' Ye Gods and Goddesses! We only got Selden's books at all by consenting to the condition that they never should be lent under any circumstances whatever; and here we have five Curators, 'all honorable men,' quietly sending off one of Selden's manuscripts to Germany. On March 21st of the same year, three Curators send off another of Selden's MSS. to London. In 1868 an application for the loan of four Hebrew manuscripts was granted, and apparently they went to a private house. On Feb. 9, 1869, two Curators, one being Dr. Pusey, 'were requested to act in the matter of the loan of Hebrew MSS. to Mr. —— of —— College, Cambridge.' On April 17 of the same year a Laudian MS. was lent to Mr. ——; there is not a syllable in the minutes about a bond, though that was absolutely necessary, nor any statement that the book was required for the purpose of publication; Laud's stipulations are quietly, and no doubt ignorantly broken under the presidency of the Vice-Chancellor. From this time loans are perpetually being made; and at least six manuscripts other than those mentioned above were lent this year. At one meeting (May 22) the whole business was the granting of loans. In 1870 fifteen MSS. at least were lent, including one of Douce's—poor fellow! he little dreamt of the fate in store for his lovely books. One MS. out of the archives was sent to Philadelphia! In 1871 some thirty manuscripts were lent; many to private hands; others to Berlin, Cambridge, and Philadelphia. Not content with these exploits, the Curators positively sent the 39th volume of the Camden Society's publications to Rouen! In 1872 nearly thirty manuscripts were lent: one 'subject to the approval of the Librarian,' thus granting to him concurrent authority with themselves. These books went some to private persons; others to Cambridge, London, Leyden, Berlin, Munster, Leipzic, Kiel, Philadelphia, and elsewhere. The manuscript sent to Munster was an old English book of Laud's; there was no bond, nor is there any hint that it was lent for publication. Besides manuscripts they lent printed books, amongst the rest Tyndale's New Testament of 1534! This portentous act was perpetrated on May 25th, 1872; and the same day there appears this entry on the minutes: 'In reference to applications for loans during the Long Vacation, it was agreed, on the suggestion of the Librarian, that he be empowered in urgent cases, with the assent of two Curators, to grant loans during the Long Vacation'; an utterly illegal resolution not rescinded till 1886.

For ten years, ever since 1862, the Curators had been lending, on their own authority, and without a shadow of statutable right, manuscripts and printed books to persons in Oxford and other parts of England, as well as to foreign countries: will it be believed that on Feb. 8, 1873, the Librarian was asked to state his opinion as to 'the lending of books out of the Library under proper restrictions;' and that on Feb. 28 of the same year, 'it was agreed that the Curators should proceed by statute to take power to order the lending out of books under certain restrictions'? Why this was the very thing they had been doing for years past; and now by agreeing 'to proceed by statute' they plainly declare their opinion that for all those years they had been doing something for which they had no statutable warrant. However, they drew up a draft statute which was laid before Council, and Council promptly 'struck out the proposal to lend books out of the Library;' whereupon on March 8th, 1873, one of the Curators moved 'that Council be requested to insert a provision that books be lent out from evening to morning. This was agreed to'. On which resolution I shall make no remark, for fear my pen might run away with me; but most people will be able to supply that comment which I refrain from making.

This very year 1873 they lent the York Missal, unless in the judgment of the Librarian 'too valuable to be lent out of the Library': there is a touch of modesty in this which disarms me, otherwise I could say something very true, but very unpleasant. The same year an application was made for one of the Douce MSS., but 'by reason of regulations as to Douce MSS. this was refused.' What regulations these were it would be interesting to know, for I cannot discover that there are at present any regulations, at all events in writing.

At length the Curators obtained their desire. On March 25, 1873, a form of statute was proposed by one Head of a House and seconded by another, and on May 2, 1873, it was carried without a division in the following shape: (Tit. XX. iii. § 11. 10.) Liceat Curatoribus, sicut mos fuit, libros impressos et manuscriptos, scientiæ causa, viris doctis sive Academicis sive externis mutuari: that is to say, Let it be lawful for the Curators, as the custom has been, to borrow books printed and manuscript in the interest of knowledge for learned men, whether Members of the University or not. A board of grave and learned men—viri variis doctrinis et literis imbuti, as the statute says—wish to do openly, what they had been in the habit of doing, as it would appear, unknown to Council, and against its wishes (for it 'struck out the proposal to lend books out of the Library'): there is something droll in that, but it is nothing to what came of it. They petition for leave to lend, walk off perfectly contented with a permission to borrow, and nobody sees the joke! 'Reform' seems not only to have impaired our knowledge of Latin, but to have diminished our sense of the ridiculous—a most dolorous result. That Convocation intended by this strangely worded statute to convey to the Curators the power to lend books is beyond question; it is equally beyond question that it conveyed the power to borrow them, for in good Latin and in our statute Latin alike, mutuari means not to lend, but to borrow, as every Latin Dictionary from the Hortus Vocabulorum down to Lewis and Short testifies; and as to our statute Latin we find: quantum magister ... potest de cista de Guildeforde mutuari (Anstey, p. 99); quod magister regens mutuari possit quadraginta solidos (ibid. p. 132); de eadem mutuari poterit ad usum suum proprium.... quinque marcas (ibid. p. 338). As mutuari is correctly used in the barbarous language of our old statutes, so is it in the more polished Latinity of the Laudian code, in which the word occurs once, and I think only once, and as the devil of mischief will have it, in the Bodleian Statute itself, where 'e cista D. Thomæ Bodley mutuari' means 'to borrow from Sir Thomas Bodley's chest'. The meaning of the word then is clear beyond dispute, and what it means in one part of the statutes it must mean in another. There is plenty of barbarous Latin in our statute book, but in every case it is justified or excused by long usage, or by the fact that other learned bodies have constantly used the same or similar language; but the statute of 1873 is probably the only one either in ancient or modern times, where without necessity, without precedent, and without warning, a word which means and always has meant one thing is used under the erroneous impression that it means another, and that not by schoolboys, but by their elders. A statute, however, means what it plainly says: with the intentions of a legislative body we have no concern except in so far as they are clearly expressed, and every prudent judge knows what grave evils spring from neglect of this principle of interpretation. (See Dwarris On Statutes, p. 580 sqq.)

Whether this statute really gives the power to lend may be disputed. On the one hand it may be said, that those who borrow a book for learned men may do what they like with it, and may therefore lend it. At first sight this seems probable and reasonable, but the more it is thought of the less probable does it appear. On the other hand it may be said, that since the statute does not plainly and expressly give the Curators the power to lend, they have no power to do so at all. Be that as it may, no such scruples troubled the minds of the Curators; every one seems to have been completely mesmerised, and this singular statute was straightway put in practice after a fashion; for on June 23, 1873, 'an application from Professor —— was considered, asking for loan of such books or MSS. as he might require, at the discretion of the Librarian, under the provisions of §11, ch. 10 of the Bodleian amended statute, during the present vacation. Mr. —— and Mr. —— made similar applications. It was agreed to accede to the request in the case of the three applicants respectively'; that is to say, within a few days of the passing of the statute it is broken. The Curators do not agree to borrow books for the applicants, the only thing the statute allowed them to do; the statute says not one word about the discretion of the Librarian, nor does it allow the Curators in this case to leave anything to it: in the buying of books (Stat. XX. iii. § 4, 4) they may leave much to his discretion, but nowhere else is any such permission given: so the Curators took it. They did not do what the statute says they may do, and they did do what no statute permits them to do; and as they began that day, so have they continued to this moment. No change is made in the minutes. Before as well as after the passing of this statute the form always is 'applications for loans,' or some equivalent phrase. In 1873 a dozen MSS. or more, besides printed books, including the Hereford Missal! were lent exactly as before, some to private persons, some to libraries, and they went to Leeds, Cambridge, Utrecht, Kiel, Berlin, andc.

In 1874 more than twenty MSS. were lent to Jena, Cambridge, Marburg, Vienna (two of the Junius collection were sent there), and to private hands. In 1875 MSS. were sent to St. Petersburg, Bonn, Vienna, Paris, Cambridge, Edinburgh, Konigsberg, Heidelberg, and some to private houses; three printed books also were lent, without a shadow of reason so far as can be seen, to a gentleman residing in the Temple.

On Oct. 30 two of the sub-librarians applied 'for the privilege of taking books out of the Library. Their application was agreed to upon the terms stated in the minutes of June 23, 1873, in the case of a similar application from others.'

And here it should be noticed that all the loans do not by any means necessarily appear in the minutes. Owing to the illegal resolution of the Curators of May 25, 1872, (see above, p. 16,) no loans during the Long Vacation are there entered. Moreover, at some time unknown to me the Librarian was quietly permitted to let certain persons borrow books at his discretion, and there at last grew up, it is to be presumed, with the knowledge of the Curators, what the Library officials call the Borrowers' List, and what after a time appears in the minutes as 'the privileged list.' As every one can see, there is nothing whatever in the statute to justify all this.

I do not for one moment mean to charge the Curators with doing anything which they thought to be improper or beyond their discretion; but I do most distinctly charge them with having in fact exceeded their statutable powers, and with taking the law into their own hands, all, I doubt not, with the best and most innocent intentions. Unfortunately some of the most mischievous acts in the world have been done with the best and purest intentions. Like all other members of the University the Curators have promised to observe the statutes, and the Vice-Chancellor and Proctors have not only done that, but have solemnly pledged themselves to see that the statutes are observed, and are moreover armed with power to enforce them. If statutes are absurd, it is clearly the duty of those who control legislation in this place to get them abolished or amended without delay; if they are not absurd, all are bound to obey them. As regards the Bodleian there is a special order (XX. iii. § 12. 3) directing the Curators what to do with an imperfect statute, and how to do it; but it is one thing to make a statute; it is a very different thing to get people to obey it. No one who sees the ease with which statutes are made and unmade, can doubt, that if those of the Bodleian are defective in any respect, it needs but a word from one or two members of Council to have all defects remedied. If the Curators want fresh powers, or more discretion, and greater latitude of action than they are at present allowed, they have but to ask and obtain; but I protest most vehemently against the usurpation of powers not granted by the University as a thing pessimi exempli. If the Bodleian Curators are to do exactly as they like, the University might just as well spare itself the trouble of legislation. If the University deliberately chooses to have its statutes nullified, there is, I suppose, no help for it; yet I cannot but suspect that the University has no knowledge—at all events no clear and distinct knowledge—of the way in which we have dealt with the statutes which were intended to mark out our duties. The secret growth of 'the borrowers' list' is as singular a thing as is to be found in the history of the Bodleian. The Curators and the Curators alone have, by a statute of their own devising, a right to borrow; yet the late Librarian assumed to himself the right of naming persons who are to have the privilege of borrowing, and the Curators quietly allowed it, without, as I believe, the faintest suspicion that they were doing what was wrong.

In 1876 eleven MSS. went some to private persons, others to Augsburg, Paris, Göttingen, Heidelberg, Cambridge: the book sent to Augsburg without bond, and without guarantee for publication, was one of Laud's Greek MSS. On June 24 an application 'from Mr. —— for use of books at home during Vacation' was 'assented to.' In 1877 some fourteen or fifteen MSS. were sent to Heidelberg, Paris, Cambridge, London, Rome, Copenhagen, Munich, Marburg, besides printed books: the book sent to Munich was one of Laud's, again in total defiance of all his stipulations.

In 1878 a dozen MSS., or more, went to different people, to Bonn, to Pesth, Leyden, and Rostock, besides printed books: one book with illuminations was refused, 'as being one of a class not lent out.' I have before observed that I know of no written rules at all. On Oct. 26 of this year the Curators surpassed themselves, for there was an application 'from the Rev. ——, Fellow of —— College, for permission to borrow works from the Library to be taken to his rooms. In this matter it was agreed that power to act on the clause 10, § 11 of the Bodleian Statute be delegated by the Curators to the Librarian.' There were ten Curators present on this memorable occasion. The Curators are themselves delegates, and if they had the right to delegate to the Librarian the power which the University delegated to them, then what is sauce for the goose is sauce for the gander: if the Curators mero motu may delegate their powers, the Librarian may with equal right and equal reason delegate his, and so on in infinitum, to the utter ruin of all sense of responsibility.

It would be tedious to enumerate all the loans; suffice it to say that they have gone on year after year; and from this point I shall only mention a few notable cases.

On May 31, 1879, 'the request of Professor —— to borrow printed books from the Library was granted.' Considering that only seven months before, the Curators had resolved 'to delegate' their lending powers to the Librarian, it is strange that they did not refer the applicant straight to that official.

In 1880, June 11, a Selden MS. was ordered to Paris; ten Curators were present, and it is to be presumed that not one of them knew, what he was bound to know, namely, the special stipulation made with respect to all Selden's books.

On Oct. 29, 1880, the Junior Proctor gave notice of the following motion:—'That in the case of MSS. sent out on loan to persons resident within the United Kingdom, a pecuniary bond shall be executed by the person to whom such MS. is lent, of such value as shall be determined from time to time by the Curators, unless the MS. is sent for use only within the precincts of the British Museum, or some other approved Public Library.' On Nov. 27 this motion was made and lost.

In 1881, June 4, 'an application from —— for the use of books dealing with the subject of Biblical Chronology at his own house appeared to the Curators to fall under the provisions of the Statute XX. iii. § 11, 10; the Librarian exercising discretion as to the number of volumes issued.' On Oct. 26, 1878, not three years before, the Curators formally 'delegated' their powers to the Librarian; on May 31, 1879, they assume that they possess what they have 'delegated'; and here they do the same thing, and all this without any formal and solemn resumption by them of their 'delegated' powers. On Oct. 29, 1881, it was reported that Professor —— of Cambridge had not returned a manuscript borrowed four years before, and the Vice-Chancellor was requested to communicate with the Professor in the matter. The manuscript never has been, and in all probability never will be restored, and our only consolation must be the fact that it was a transcript of another manuscript in the Bodleian, not on that account necessarily of little value, for a transcript may, and sometimes does, become of inestimable value; why it does so, all acquainted with books know.

In 1882, Feb. 11, a Laudian MS. was ordered to Heidelberg, and a Selden MS. to St. Petersburg. On Dec. 2, 1882, 'it was agreed that Mr. ——, Fellow of —— be one of the persons privileged to take out books. It was agreed that the Librarians be allowed to take out books and MSS. for their own use.'

In 1883, Jan. 27, the Librarian suggested 'that all Fellows and ex-Fellows of Colleges should be entitled to have books out of the Library'; the suggestion was not adopted. On the same day, 'Mr. —— (—— College) and Dr. —— were placed on the list of persons specially entitled.' On March 3 of the same year, 'Dr. Frankfurter's application to be placed on the privileged list of borrowers was assented to.' There we have it at last, in black and white—the privileged list of borrowers, as unstatutable and as illegal a thing as could well be permitted. The words 'let it be lawful for the Curators to borrow books for learned men,' (always supposing the Latin not to be downright nonsense,) cannot convey to the Curators the power to let other people borrow books; for if they could, then any words may have any meaning, which comes to the same thing as saying that they have no meaning at all. Yet it is on these words, and on these words alone, that the 'borrowers' list' has been made to depend; though how educated men can have extracted from this statute any meaning whatever which would justify, or even seem, in the most distant way, to justify the act of conveying to others the power to borrow books from the library is one of the most astonishing things that I ever met with in the whole course of my life. But it will be said that the Bodleian Curators for thirteen years understood mutuari to mean 'lend', and therefore they might institute a 'borrowers' list'. It is an astonishing, not to say staggering, fact that they did so understand it, yet the borrowers' list is none the less illegal. Nay, I have heard a Curator in his place maintain, that as there could be no doubt what the University intended when it passed this statute, mutuari in this place must mean 'lend'. Much as I admired the boldness of the assertion, I was unable to commend either the law or the logic of it; the consequences which would at once follow from the position, that if the intentions of a legislative body are clear it matters not how it expresses them, are too palpably absurd to find acceptance with ordinary minds. However, let it be supposed, that instead of mutuari the word actually used were commodare. You are still no better off. The University on this hypothesis gives to the Curators as a board the power of lending a specific book to a specific person, and that is all. It does not give the Curators the power to invest any person or persons with the right or privilege of borrowing books, still less does it convey the power of creating a class of persons who have such a right or privilege. This is not only clear to plain common sense, but, as I am advised, is plain as a matter of law; and I am further assured that, if any book is damaged or lost in consequence of the Curators persisting in such a course, they become themselves personally liable to the University.

This illegal borrowers' list comprises at this moment (subtracting one dead man and double entries) one hundred and eleven persons, besides the Clarendon Press. Among these persons are two ladies, who can have no conceivable right to be where they are, for even those whose tolerant Latinity suffers them to take mutuari for commodare will hardly maintain that 'viris doctis' covers learned women. It includes too non-residents and foreigners; and I am informed that manuscripts have been sent for the use of one of these persons more than a hundred miles as the crow flies. Books are sent by post, and Bodleian money is spent to pay for carriage. The finances of the Library, however, deserve a paper all to themselves, and some day they shall have one.

On May 26, 1883, 'an application from Dr. Leumann to be placed on the privileged list was agreed to.' On Oct. 20, of the same year, two persons were 'placed on the privileged list of readers;' and on Nov. 24, another 'was placed on the privileged list;' and from that moment to the present no other formula is employed in the minutes.

In 1885, Oct. 31, the Librarian applied 'for authority to decline requests for loans of Selden MSS. and books, and of Laud's MSS. (except for purposes of publication), without referring the application to the Curators, as being contrary to the terms of the respective donations. This was agreed to.' It was, and to my great astonishment it passed without any remark whatever.

In 1886, March 13, 'Liceat Curatoribus' was ruled to mean 'the consent of a majority of Curators;' that is to say, the illegal resolution of May 25, 1872, was silently rescinded. On May 15 of the same year a committee of four was appointed to consider the practice of loans. At a meeting on June 19, another name was added to the borrowers' list. Every Curator knew that the legality of their practice with respect to loans, and especially with respect to the borrowers' list, had been openly challenged; notwithstanding this, and in spite of protest then and there made, the chairman put the name to the vote, and a majority actually voted for it. This proceeding was, in my opinion (and not in mine only), irregular and improper to say the least of it, but it was highly characteristic. After waiting to see whether the Vice-Chancellor or any other Curator would call attention to the charge brought against the board, and finding, as I was sure would be the case, that no one shewed any disposition to do so, I gave notice of a motion for the next statutable meeting:—That the borrowers' list be abolished as illegal; that all books in the hands of borrowers be at once recalled as having been illegally lent; and that for the future the Statute XX. iii. § 11. 10 be faithfully observed.

On June 28 it was agreed (I being silent for an obvious reason) that during the Vacation all the Curators in Oxford should meet every fortnight in the Library at 2 p.m. solely to consider applications for loans. During the Vacation six such meetings were summoned. On July 10, three Curators met and refused an application; on Aug. 21, and on Sept. 11, only two were present, and of course declined to act; on Sept. 25, and Oct. 9, I, who attended all the meetings, found myself alone; on Oct. 23, there were six of us, and business was adjourned on the ground that the whole question of loans would be debated on Oct. 30. Accordingly, on Oct. 30, all the Curators made their appearance, a thing I never saw before, though they were not all present during the whole of the proceedings. The motion to abolish the borrowers' list was duly made and seconded; then, after some confused talk, which could not be dignified by the name of a debate, an amendment was moved, 'That the consideration of the regulations under which books be lent be referred to a committee'; and this was carried, all the Curators being present. An instruction to the committee was also moved, 'To consider what alteration is required in the statute with regard to the borrowing of books'; which was also carried. Next we considered the report of the committee on loans, and returned it in a somewhat mangled condition to the reconsideration of those who drew it up. After that, applications for loans numbered 1 to 16 were discussed, and all were refused. This exhausted the agenda paper, and should, I apprehend, have finished the business of the day. However, an application for the loan of manuscripts not on the agenda paper was considered, and the board, which up to that moment had refused all applications, including one from Sir Richard Burton, granted the loan of seventeen manuscripts to one man. In self-defence, let me say that I always vote against all loans when there is a division.

On Nov. 8 the loan committee recommended that Council be asked to propose amendments in Stat. Tit. XX. sect. iii. § 11, and thought that 'the farther consideration of the rules framed by them and amended at the Curators' meeting on Oct. 30 should for the present be postponed.' On Nov. 25, ten Curators being present, this recommendation was considered. One of the Curators thought that while there was 'no harm' in applying for a new statute, yet that it was 'a waste of time' and 'a little ridiculous': another wished to move an amendment and have the new statute in English, but some of us saw (though no one said so) that such an amendment would be a highly comic confession on the part of the viri variis doctrinis et literis imbuti; and accordingly it was not pressed. Then the same Curator proposed that commodare should be substituted for mutuari, and that sicut mos fuit should be struck out. Four voted for this amendment, which was lost. Even had it been carried, it would still have been unlawful to lend books to women, for, as was pointed out at the time, vir means a man; but the minority was in no mood to be affected by philological facts. The original recommendation was then passed.

The board having thus expressed its opinion that a new statute was necessary to enable it to lend books had, it might be thought, asserted that the existing statute does not enable it to do so; accordingly we at once turned our attention to applications for loans. The first article applied for was not a book at all, but an inscribed bronze vessel; and it was observed that we have no statutable right, in other words no power whatever, to lend such a thing; whereupon some one remarked that it might be done, because it is not forbidden, an argument, which (if valid) would lead to some startling conclusions.

However, that a decree of Convocation to authorise the loan of this vessel should be asked for was duly moved and seconded; then the Curator, who wished to patch the Bodleian Latin statute with a bit of English, moved as an amendment 'that the Curators lend it', quite ignoring the fact that they had no statutable power to do so. For this amendment three Curators voted, one abstained, and the rest voted against it: finally the original motion was carried. After that, two loans of books were refused and three were granted.

In applying for a decree to enable them to lend this vessel the Curators turned over a new leaf. The whole Bodleian statute consists of ten octavo pages, eleven lines and four words: it can be read out aloud in thirty minutes, and by eye alone in half that time: there is, therefore, no excuse whatever for not knowing its contents, and still less for not obeying it. It is not my purpose at the present moment to point out how often, and in how many ways, we drive a coach and four through statutes intended to control our actions; but to complete the subject of loans, and dismissing the practice of book-lending from further consideration, it may be noted that the Stat. XX. iii. § 11. 9 allows the Curators under specified conditions to place certain prints and drawings either in the Radcliffe or in the Taylor Building; but with this exception, if exception it be, no power is anywhere given to them to lend any picture, coin, antiquity, or other object belonging to the library. Nevertheless I find the following entries in the minutes:—

On April 26, 1865, 'it was agreed to lend "Miniatures" to the Lords of the Committee of Council on Education to be exhibited in the South Kensington Museum.'

On Oct. 28, 1865, 'the Curators sanction the loan of such Pictures as may be desired for the National Exhibition of Portraits at Kensington in 1866.'

On Dec. 12, 1865, 'that the loan of the Pictures according to the list sent, save that of Sir Thomas Bodley, be granted to South Kensington Museum Exhibition of National Portraits.'

On March 8, 1867, 'a letter from the Secretary of the Earl of Derby was read asking for the loan of eighteen Pictures for exhibition at Kensington. This was acceded to.'

On Jan. 31, 1868, 'it was resolved ... to lend to the Leeds Exhibition the Portraits they wish of Yorkshire Worthies.'

On Feb. 5, 1870, 'an application from Mr. Cosmo Innis, of the General Register house, Edinburgh, for the loan of the old map of Britain of the 14th century, which hangs on the wall of the Library, to be traced in facsimile, under the care of Sir Henry James, for the 2nd volume of the National MSS. of Scotland, was granted.'

On Feb. 14, 1874, 'an application from the South Kensington Museum was read, asking for the loan of remarkable specimens of Book-binding for next year's International Exhibition. In this matter it was agreed that the Museum should be invited to send a person to Oxford to inspect, and that it should be left to the discretion of the Librarian to decide upon lending any specimen required.'

On April 28, 1877, 'an application from Mr. Bladeson behalf of Caxton memorial committee for the loan of certain early printed books to a Public Exhibition at South Kensington was considered and granted.'

On May 26, 1877, application 'for Bibles to be sent to the Caxton Exhibition. This was granted, and the Librarian was directed to take such measures as might be necessary to ensure secure transmission.'

On May 11, 1878, permission was given to lend the Selden Portrait to the Nottingham Art Exhibition; and an application from the Bath and West of England Agricultural Society for works of art, andc. for their approaching meeting at Oxford, was considered. This was left to the Librarian's discretion.

On Nov. 13, 1880, Wyngarde's Plan of London 'to be granted under a bond' to Mr. Wheatley.

On April 29, 1882, the Portrait of Sam. Butler was lent to the Worcestershire Exhibition of Fine Arts.

On Feb. 2, 1884, Drake's Chair was lent to the Mayor of Plymouth.

On May 2, 1885, 'the Librarian presented applications from the Exhibition of Inventions now being held for the loan of certain MSS.; certain early printed books; certain works on music. It was agreed that the Librarian be empowered to lend out of the above as required, as he may think well, to the Exhibition.'

At this last meeting I was present, and the following is a verbatim copy of my note written the same day:—

'An Exhibition of Inventions (I have not got the name correctly) applied for the loan of certain MSS. and books from Bodleian: 5 MSS. Liturgies: 3 Bodley MSS. 515, 775, 842: Gough, Missal 336: an Ashmole book, and 2 English.—I objected, but the loan was carried, except as to 775 Bodley.' I have lately been informed that one of the books sent up to be stared at by the mob of sightseers was a Selden book: this I neither knew nor could have known at the time, or it should have been stopped, if protesting could have stopped it.

In every one of these cases the Curators, with the most perfect innocence, took upon themselves to do what they had not a shadow of right to do. If the University is content to have its property so dealt with that in case of damage or loss its only remedy would be to mulct the Curators, there is nothing more to be said; but it is just as well that the University should know what has been done in the past, and what would have been done in the future, had not a protest been made against the practice; and even now, though the board as a board has seemingly condemned its former doings, it still contains a stubborn and impenitent minority. If the University wishes its statutes to be obeyed, it should ordain substantial pecuniary fines for breaches of them; if it does not care whether they are obeyed or not, it is a pity that it wastes its time in enacting them.

And now as to the policy of lending the printed books and manuscripts of the Bodleian. The question is not whether it is a good or a bad thing to lend books, nor whether it is a good thing for this or that library to do so; it is simply whether it is right to lend Bodleian books. It may be argued that it is right to do so—

1. Because books are made to be used, and they will be very much more used if they are lent than if they are not; moreover it is generally more convenient to read in one's own room than it is in a public place. Some men cannot read, certainly cannot read and think in a library, or in the midst of company; I cannot myself, and all that I have ever been able to do in such places is to make extracts, verify references and the like; but to read a book as I should in my own room is to me, and probably to many people, impossible. If you go to a public institution you must go when it is open; you must sit still; you must not whistle or make a noise; you must not smoke; you cannot lie down and read on your back; you cannot throw the book aside, go for a walk, and resume your perusal; you cannot read quietly over the fire of an evening; you cannot read in the small hours of the night, and so on ad infinitum. Yet all this you can do if you are allowed to borrow the books. You can then treat them exactly as if they were your own. It is clear that this argument may be expanded in a multitude of ways, and no one is so destitute of imagination as not to be able to fill up the details to suit his own particular case and fancy.

The answer to it is very simple. You cannot by any device or contrivance combine the advantages of private and of public property. He who wishes to use the books of a public library must submit to many personal inconveniences; and the man who is unwilling to deny himself for the general good is the very last person in the community to whom any favour ought to be shown, and of all people he least deserves the favour of borrowing. He who has ever been foolish enough to lend his own books freely, learns by almost unvaried experience that hardly one man in twenty can be trusted: your book comes back (when it comes back at all) more damaged by a month's outing than the owner would occasion in fifty years. The book of a public library is even less regarded, as a rule, than that belonging to a friend; for the friend may have a sharp tongue, and a knack of using it, whereas a librarian is an official; even if he ever has time to look through the books when they are returned, his censure is disregarded, and after all accidents will happen, and the book might possibly have been equally damaged had it never left the library walls. It is really astonishing how few men there are in the present day who know how to use a book without doing it real and often serious damage. Over and over again have I seen men who would be very angry to be called boors deliberately break the back of a book. Over and over again, both in libraries and in private rooms, have I seen the headband broken, simply because people did not know how to take a book off a shelf. Again and again I have seen men of education (but grossly ignorant for all that of the ways of books) play such pranks with my own volumes as made me shudder. The horrid trick of turning a leaf by wetting a finger I have seen practised in this seat of learning over and over again by Graduates, by Professors, by Heads of Houses; and years ago I saw that same nasty trick played pro pudor! in the sacred precincts of the Bodleian itself on a manuscript, which will bear to its last moment the impression of the dirty thumb (and it was dirty) that perpetrated the uncleanly act. Often and often you see a man sitting close over the fire with a well-bound volume; a few such experiments will ruin the binding of any book; if it is his own, well and good, though even so the act is that of a barbarian: but suppose it a Bodleian book, what then? Why in that case the binding bills will be higher than ever, to say nothing about the ruin of the book itself. A man who knows how to handle a book will use a volume habitually for years and leave no trace of wear and tear behind him; but the average man, even though he may be a Master of Arts, is, not unfrequently, totally unfit to have the use of any books in good condition, even in a library, much less out of one.

The scholars and readers of former days seem to have been far more careful in their habits than men are now. Look at the books of the great collectors—Grolier, the Maioli, Selden, De Thou, the Colberts, and the like. These men read their books; and Grolier and Thomas Maioli certainly lent them: yet even after all these years, though time and neglect may have ruined the magnificent bindings—bindings such as few, if any, modern collectors ever indulge in—the books themselves are internally spotless. I have myself scores of volumes, many of them three or four hundred years old, clean and pure as the day they were issued from the press; they have most certainly been used and read, but used by men of clean hands and decent habits. In the present day books are so common and so cheap, and modern readers too frequently so unrefined, that they get into a vile habit of misusing them, and to such persons—that is, to the great majority—the books of a public library cannot be safely trusted except under the very strictest supervision. The slovenly practice of placing one open book on another, a practice sternly forbidden in many foreign libraries, may be seen in full swing both at the Camera and in the Bodleian; and no one seems to be aware how ruinous it is, or to have the least suspicion that he who knows how to handle books never treats them so. Treated in a cleanly and decent manner, there is not the least reason why a book printed on good paper should not last for twenty centuries or more; treated as they are too often treated here in Oxford, they will hardly last as many months.

By lending the books as we illegally do, we are perceptibly hastening the destruction of a library intended by its founder and benefactors to be a blessing for generations of scholars yet unborn.

2. Books are to be lent, and what is more ought to be sent out of Oxford, because it is an immense convenience to students at a distance to have Bodleian treasures close at hand. Not a doubt about it; vastly convenient. Suppose I am studying Greek sculpture, it would be very convenient to get all the master-pieces sent from the various galleries of Europe to London or Oxford. It would not only be a convenience, but a joy and a delight, to have over the Venus of Melos. Instead of sitting for hours together, as I used to do, in the Louvre, it would be much more convenient to go down to the New Schools and gaze on that glorious and divine being. Does any one suddenly scent an absurdity in the supposition? Why so do I, but the absurdity is in the whole argument, not in the particular application of it. Some people who have not a gift for seeing the point of things will ride off by saying that the Venus is a majestic beauty, and that the expense of her carriage and insurance would be enormous. Such an objection is pointless, because it evades the question of convenience; but let us take a case where weight will not oppress us. Say you study Greek gems; would it not be very convenient to have some of the best from Naples, from Paris, from Rome, and from Vienna, sent here to the Bodleian, where you could study them at your leisure? They are more portable than books, far less liable to damage, and hardly more valuable. Do you think that any guardian of such treasures would be so foolish as to listen to your request? Would any nation, city, or even University, permit it?

The cases, it will be said, are not parallel. Gems, coins, medals, statuettes, are too valuable to be lent; the books and manuscripts which the Bodleian Curators lend are comparatively valueless. I am by no means sure of that fact. I have before now tapped at a friend's door, and receiving no answer entered his room to leave a message or what not, and have more than once seen lying on his table an eleventh-century Bodleian manuscript of a certain classic author, a book of inestimable value, the codex archetypus of every other copy now in existence. Any stranger could have entered that room, and any enterprising literary thief—a not uncommon and particularly detestable animal—might have slipped this priceless book into his pocket. I am by no means sure that very valuable manuscripts have not been, in spite of remonstrance, lent out within the last two years; but it is beyond all dispute that not so very long ago the thing was done, and any man or any body of men who will allow one such thing to be done are quite capable of allowing a dozen to be done.

Let it, however, be granted, for the purposes of the present argument, that we now, having a clearer perception of our responsibilities, only allow comparatively worthless manuscripts to be sent to France, to Germany, Russia, or India; for our manuscripts, be it observed, travel as far afield as Bombay. Now what makes a book or manuscript comparatively worthless?

31

It is so, either because it is one of many copies, or because it is a poor and faulty copy. If it is one of many, why in the name of all that is absurd should we be asked to send our goods away (at our expense and risk let it be remembered) when ex hypothesi there are many other copies in existence? why cannot the foreign student go to some one of those copies? why should we be called on to gratify his laziness or consult his convenience? If the copy be a poor one, he who asks for the loan of it must be a noodle, for who cares for the readings of a confessedly inferior book? Is it not clear as day that the man who at Rome, or Heidelberg, or Bombay, asks for the loan of a manuscript, believes it to be a good and valuable copy? moreover, if he believes so, is it not in the highest degree probable that his judgment is correct, seeing that his attention is in a special manner concentrated on the matter? And if it be a good and valuable copy, what becomes of the plea that we only lend comparatively worthless books? Have we any common sense amongst us? I really confess that there are times when I come to the conclusion that we have none; for if we had, how could we be deceived by pretexts so flimsy and fallacious? All the manuscripts which we now lend are most certainly valuable, and their loss or damage would be irreparable; all talk of comparative worth or worthlessness is futile, and is merely used as so much dust thrown in the eyes of those who (I am sorry to say it, but it must be said) ought to have a higher conception of their duties.

3. Some maintain that MSS. and books should be lent out because 'more work' will be done by that device. It is difficult to see why. It is inferred, in fact, that 'more work' will be done, because it is more convenient to work at home than it is in a library. A partial answer to this fallacious plea has been already given, but I cannot pass over the particular form of it without a protest. The cant that is talked now-a-days about 'work' is enough to make one sick. As far as my experience extends, the very notion of work, as opposed to fidgetty pottering, is not possessed by fifty men in the place; the very conception of thoroughness and comprehension is gone; and as to learning, why the thing has almost vanished; of 'science' we have enough and to spare, but what in the world has become of all our knowledge? Briefly, at the present moment and in this place, all this wretched pretence of 'work' is arrant imposture. A few, and only a few, know what it means, and they would never dream of talking about it.

But I have heard this argument about 'more work' put in another form, and it obviously is a theme on which endless variations may be composed. Suppose, it is said, a very poor scholar, anxious to give the world a critical edition of some book, and further suppose that there is a valuable manuscript at St. Petersburg, another at Stockholm, another in Paris, another in Oxford, and so on; let the poor scholar live where you like, say in Giessen, and suppose him to be totally unable to defray the expense of a journey to these several places, and to have no means of paying for collations made by others, and no confidence in their correctness, even if he could pay for them; would it not be an advantage to literature that all these manuscripts should be sent to Giessen for the use of the poor scholar aforesaid; and would it not be a dead loss to the world of letters, if, by refusing so to lend them, you prevented the poor scholar from constructing a critical and admirable text of the author in whom he is interested? This purely hypothetical case I have heard put in all seriousness, and used as a knock-me-down sort of argument; yet it must occur to any one with a grain of common sense that it is only too easy to 'suppose' anything; that it would not require the imaginative powers of a baby to go one step further, and suppose the poor, the ardent and the ripe scholar to have just money enough or pluck enough to carry him to the places which he wishes to visit, (I note parenthetically that a real student, a man to read of whose exploits warms one's heart, Cosma de Körös, started on his extraordinary expedition to the East with 100 florins and a walking-stick, for being what he was, he dispensed with luggage,) or you might suppose brains enough in his neighbourhood to perceive that so deserving a creature of the pure imagination might fairly enough be helped or—but it is needless and foolish to dream with one's eyes open, and practical men generally object to discuss purely hypothetical cases. Yes, my excellent but fanciful friend will say, this is all very well, but if there were such a case, what would you do? Well, to speak for myself, I should prefer to wait till the poor scholar's exchequer was in a more flourishing condition, or why should I not take a turn at 'supposing' myself? and perform the very easy trick of imagining a more ripe scholar, a more enthusiastic student, endowed not only with brains, but blessed with means to gratify his whims, and then, without the least violence, I might suppose the result to be a much more correct, a much more critical edition than my friend's phantom scholar could ever by any possibility concoct. But to return to the region of reality; I answer that not even in the case supposed, or in any case would I lend out manuscripts, and this for more reasons than I have patience to write down. One remark may, however, be made. We are constantly requested to send manuscripts abroad 'for collation,' and we not unfrequently send them. Will any one be good enough to mention to me a single collation of a Greek or Latin classic made by any scholar by profession of any manuscript of fair length—say, if you like, 300 pages of octavo print—which is faithful, or which can be depended on? Even if it were a defensible practice to send manuscripts abroad for collation, it can never be a defensible practice to expose them to all the risks they necessarily run, and after all reap as a net result collations not worth the paper they are written on.

I hope that these considerations may satisfy my imaginative friend that there is not that force in his argument which he supposes; but if he is still unconvinced, let us agree to consider the case of the poor scholar when it actually occurs on its merits, and let it be conceded as a thing not impossible, that should all the supposed conditions exist, we might for once in a way move Convocation to lend a manuscript for the use of so singular and so deserving a character; how does that justify us in sending manuscripts abroad when no such conditions exist? The most I have ever yet heard pleaded on behalf of these foreign students was, not that they could not afford to come to Oxford, but merely that it was much more convenient to have a book sent out to Hungary or Russia, than it was for the Hungarian or Russian to visit us. I dare say it was more convenient to him, but it has already been observed that he who wishes to use public property must and ought to submit to not a few personal inconveniences. It would, too, be interesting to know whether, supposing any of us possessed a very valuable book of our own, we should be ready and willing to lend it as freely as we lend these books which are not ours. I will answer for myself that I certainly should not, and that it would be grossly inconsistent in me to lend University property when I decline under precisely similar circumstances to lend my own.

4. Again, it is argued that since foreign libraries are willing to lend to us we ought to reciprocate their liberality: we ought, it is said, to be as liberal as France or Germany are. To the end of time men will be the dupes of phrases and the slaves of words, yet it is a little strange that we, who fancy ourselves in some respects raised above the mob, should see any force in this singular perversion of language. Who does not detect the hollow and worthless nature of that 'liberality' which lends, not what is its own, but what is another's? In what possible sense, except an illusory and fallacious one, can the Bodleian Curators credit themselves with the virtue of 'liberality' when they hand over, not their own property, not anything which they collectively set great store on, not anything which it would grieve them deeply to lose, but something not their own? Such liberality seems to me to be as cheap as it is worthless; as easy as it is unreal. But, it will be objected, that the University empowers them so to lend, and that it would be 'illiberal' in them to accept loans from others and refuse themselves to lend. As to the powers given by the University, I have already said something; the rest of the plea may be sufficiently answered by a single line from Hamlet—
"Neither a borrower nor a lender be."

Sound, wholesome advice to all, whether taken as Polonius intended it, or as I now use it. It would be mean and shabby to borrow if you refuse to lend, for it would be conniving at a vice which you decline to commit. Would it not be more rational to argue that all lending out of Bodleian books being bad, we therefore decline to benefit (if benefit it be) by a practice which we disapprove of in principle? To argue simply, as I have heard some do, that because foreign libraries are willing to lend us books, therefore we ought to be willing to lend them books, is, as an argument, about as valid as it would be to say, 'My friend X has signified his willingness to lend me his banjo, and therefore I am bound to lend him my Erard's piano, if he asks for it': not every one would see the force of such reasoning. If the lending of books from such a library as the Bodleian be, as I maintain it is, bad in principle, it can never become right because other libraries are willing to be loose in their practice.

But suppose we look a little more closely into this alleged 'liberality' of foreign countries, where lending in some form or other is the rule rather than the exception. And here let it be observed that 'library' though one word covers things as different as chalk is from cheese. Libraries differ not merely in quantity, in the number of volumes which they contain: they also differ enormously in quality and value. The University Library of Göttingen some forty years ago was estimated to contain 350,000 volumes. The Grenville Library (now part of the British Museum) consists in round numbers of 20,000 volumes, each of which cost on an average two pounds, fourteen shillings; and this small but most choice collection would in the present day probably sell for a sum almost sufficient to purchase the whole of the Göttingen 350,000 volumes. The Bodleian is equalled and even far surpassed in point of numbers by other libraries, but for quality and real value there are not in all the world a dozen that could, or by any competent person would, be compared with it, and this fact makes all the difference when lending is in question. You might lend and lose half the books at Göttingen, and still be able without very much trouble or expense to replace them to the satisfaction of that University. By losing a single half-dozen of some of our Bodleian books, you might seriously maim and cripple a large department; and as to replacing the half-dozen, you might just as well try to replace the coal in our coal pits. I have seen it stated that all the great libraries of Europe lend, except the Vatican and the British Museum: even Mr. Panizzi, forgetting for the moment what he well knew, says, 'In all libraries on the Continent they lend books, but here [i.e. at the British Museum] I hope they will never lend them: it is quite right not to lend them' (Report on British Museum, 1850, p. 230). And even if all do lend (and all do not), it would no more follow that they ought to do so, than it follows that no man should do right, because all men are sinners. Why are we to follow a foreign fashion? Why are we to follow a multitude to do evil? We are quite strong enough to act properly, if we only had the infinitesimal amount of courage needful. Even if it were true that every great library in Europe does a foolish thing, why should we, with the true spirit of slavish imitation, be equally foolish?

Amongst the libraries, which may be with more or less justice compared with the Bodleian, are the National Library of Paris; the British Museum; the Vatican; the Royal Library of Munich; the Imperial Library of St.

Petersburg; the Imperial Library at Vienna; the Ambrosian at Milan. Thirty odd years ago only two of these ever lent a book, and then hardly in the sense in which any one in Oxford would understand that phrase. At this very moment, the British Museum, the second or third largest and finest library in the world, does not lend; the Vatican does not lend; the Ambrosian library, great in printed books, greater in manuscripts, does not lend; the Escurial, famed for its Arabic manuscripts, never lends, not even within the limits of Spain; the Municipal Library of Ravenna, a name well known to all students of Aristophanes for its famous codex, never lends; nor does the Angelica at Rome: and there are more libraries of which this is true. Few, however, would believe till they have tried the experiment, how difficult it is for a private person to get really trustworthy information as to the practices of foreign libraries.

Again, all foreign libraries that practise lending lend under restrictions unknown to us in Oxford. At the Bodleian there are no written rules at all, and, as far as I know, there never have been any. The present Librarian rightly felt that such a state of things ought not to be allowed; he accordingly drew up a draft set of regulations; it was at his request that the committee mentioned above, p. 26, was appointed, and but for his sense of duty the board would possibly never have perceived that rules were requisite. The Italian government controls some 33 libraries, and the rules for loans fill 83 paragraphs and 18 pages quarto. Without the special leave of the Minister of Instruction, no government librarian in Italy can lend manuscripts, printed books of the 15th century, very rare editions, books with autographs of celebrated men or with important notes, books printed on vellum, books with plates of much value, or the chief value of which consists in the engravings, expensive works, works in many volumes, coast surveys, maps, atlases, books finely bound or otherwise valuable, old music. In other words, no librarian can lend any manuscript whatever, or any valuable printed book, without special leave. The restrictions on loans to foreign countries are also numerous.

The National Library of Paris, the largest in the whole world, also lends, but never in the wild fashion sanctioned in this place. Here are the very words of the 'Règlement,' Art. 115: 'Peuvent seuls être prêtés dans le département des imprimés, les doubles qui ne font pas partie de la réserve, pourvu, en outre, qu'il ne s'agisse ni de livres particulièrement précieux, ni de dictionnaires, ni de journaux, ni de morceaux ou partitions de musique, ni de volumes appartenant à de grandes collections ou contenant des figures hors texte.

'Ne peuvent pas non plus être prêtés les romans, ni les pièces du théâtre moderne, ni les ouvrages de littérature frivole. Le conservateur apprécie en premier ressort les circonstances qui permettent ou non de prêter un livre.'

Art. 116: 'Peuvent seuls être prêtés dans le département des manuscrits, les volumes qui ne sont pas particulièrement précieux par leur rareté, leur antiquité, les autographes ou les miniatures qu'ils contiennent, ou par toute autre circonstance dont le conservateur est juge en premier ressort.'

This library then never lends anything but duplicates, and only such duplicates as are not part of the reserve, i.e. part of the more valuable section of the library, and not even such duplicates if they are specially valuable.

The libraries of Germany and Switzerland have rules substantially the same as those adopted in France and Italy; and it is the same with Belgium when they lend at all. In the Bibliothèque Royale de Belgique, Art. 41 of the 'Règlement' runs thus: 'Dans la section des imprimés, les ouvrages d'un usage journalier, les livres rares, de luxe ou à figures, les éditions du XVe siècle, les livres sur vélin ou sur grand papier, ceux dont les reliures sont précieuses ou remarquables, les collections ou parties de collection considérable ne sont jamais prêtés au dehors.'

As to the Imperial Library of St. Petersburg, the Director writes under date Dec. 11, 1886: 'la Bibliothèque Impériale n'a pas le droit, d'après la loi, de prêter ses manuscrits aux personnes particulières, que sur la demande des autorités compètents, et pour les personnes hors des limites de la Russie, que par l'entremise du ministère des affaires étrangères avec l'autorisation de Sa Majesté. En même temps je crois devoir ajouter, que les manuscrits les plus précieux ne sortent jamais de la Bibliothèque, dans aucun cas, de même que les codes dont s'occupent les savants du pays.'

It would be impossible to do in any of these foreign countries what is done in Oxford. Expensive illustrated works are, as I have heard, had out of the library, and are then used to illustrate lectures—a short and easy method of bringing books to ruin.

To trust to discretion alone, whether it be the discretion of a librarian or of a board, is to lean on a broken reed; and in most foreign libraries that discovery has long since been made: it is high time that we made it too, if we are foolish enough to sanction the practice of lending.

When it is said then that all great foreign libraries lend, let it always be remembered, in the first place, that strictly speaking all do not lend; and, in the second place, that those which lend restrict the practice in a way never dreamt of here.

Such then are the arguments for lending: they may be stated in other terms, and they may be indefinitely varied in shape, but when reduced to their ultimate forms they simply come to this—that by lending books out the utility of the library is increased, the convenience of readers is consulted, the progress of learning is facilitated, and international courtesy is promoted—all very good things in themselves and much to be desired, but, as always in this world, we have to balance good with evil, and to take that course which involves the least inconvenience on the whole.

I confess that it rather depresses me to have to argue the question at all, and if the genius loci affected all minds as it affects mine, the very faintest suspicion of degrading and vulgarising such an institution as the Bodleian would be enough, and more than enough, to settle the matter; and surely it is a degradation of that noble library to look on it, as some seem to do, as a sort of enlarged and diversified Mudie's. Our books may be all over Oxford, nay, all over Europe; they may be in Germany, in France, in India, in Russia, in London, at Cambridge, and heaven only knows where. What is all this but the first step towards turning the Bodleian into a vast and vulgar circulating library? I must say again, as I have said elsewhere, that the Bodleian Library is absolutely unlike any other library in the world; it is in its way peerless and unique; it was founded and augmented by learned men for learned men; it was never meant for the motley crew which in the present day crams the Camera and the Library itself. It is sad to one who can remember what the Bodleian was even thirty years ago to see such rapid decline, such manifest tokens of disregard for all that once rendered the place a sacred spot. But this is to wander from my immediate business, and what I conceive to be the abuse, I might even say the gross abuse of the Bodleian, for which the Curators are directly responsible, must be matter for some other paper.

It seems to be the notion of some people in this University that the Bodleian Library is a fit place for readers of any and of every kind. They have not knowledge enough of books or of libraries to see that a library suitable only to scholars of a high class is not a library adapted to learners and schoolboys.

Any one beginning microscopic work will find all, and more than all, his wants satisfied for a long time to come by a five guinea instrument, and he is not unlikely to damage even that. Suppose that, instead of such an instrument, you gave him at once a two hundred pound microscope by Smith and Beck, or Ross, what would happen? He would be utterly bewildered by the complexity of it, utterly unable to use it as it should be used, and he would most certainly before long so damage it as to render it useless to all who could make a proper use of it. Between a first-rate microscope by Ross and a three or five guinea instrument the difference is much less than is the difference between the Bodleian and a library fit for undergraduates, or generally for the unlearned. By introducing undergraduates, schoolboys, and girls into such a library as the Bodleian, you in fact degrade the library to base uses, and render it pro tanto inconvenient, to use a very mild term, to all who are fit to benefit by it, and who were intended by the founder to have the advantage of it.

'What my experience has taught me,' says a most learned bibliographer (1. R. 121)[15], 'is, that it ought never to be attempted to use, as a popular library, the large libraries intended in the first instance for a superior class of readers;' and he adds further, that 'on every occasion, when it has been tried, the greatest part of the riches accumulated in the old library have been rendered useless.'

[15] Report from the Select Committee on Public Libraries, ordered by the House of Commons to be printed 23 July, 1849, quoted by pages as 1. R. A second volume ordered to be printed 1 August, 1850, is quoted also by pages as 2. R. These Blue books contain an immense amount of information on all the libraries of Europe, and although the information is some forty years old, it is still indispensable to all who wish to acquaint themselves with the subject. The evidence also given is of the most varied kind, and very instructive.

If it is in any sense useful to lend books out of the library, it is far more useful, all things considered, not to lend them.

Every man of the least intelligence can see the difference between a library of reference and one from which books are lent. A library of reference, or a library of deposit, is one where books are to be perpetually preserved as carefully as may be for the convenience of scholars and students, and for the promotion of sound and solid learning; and lending any book from such a library is obviously inconsistent with the very purpose for which it is founded. 'I think,' says the Solicitor-General for Scotland, speaking of the Advocates' Library, 'that (lending books out) is quite inconsistent with the proper preservation of a great library' (1. R. 95).[16] And another very able witness, Mr. Colles, one of the library committee of the Royal Dublin Society, gives it as the result of his experience that no lending should be allowed in such a library. 'I speak,' he says, 'against the interest of my own family when I say this: but I think that the public use of the library would be increased by not lending.' And again, 'The two (i. e. libraries of reference and of circulation) ought to be separated, just as banks of issue should be separated from banks of deposit. I wish to be understood on this point: an individual painter or sculptor might be greatly benefited by borrowing out a capital picture from the National Gallery, or the Torso, Venus, or Portland Vase from the British Museum; but such a loan would by no means benefit artists in general, or advance the ultimate interests of painting or sculpture. This holds good equally with regard to valuable books.' (1. R. 185.)

[16] See note 15, p. 46.

This question as to the expediency of lending books out of such libraries as the British Museum or the Bodleian has been hotly debated both at home and abroad for the last eighty years or more, and I wish I had space to detail the arguments that have been used, not by men ignorant of books and eager only to consult their own convenience, or to obtain credit for a spurious liberality; but by those who really and truly knew all the ins and outs of the matter they were talking about, and who were quite as anxious to promote learning as we are ourselves. Take, for instance, the late Mr. Thomas Watts, keeper of printed books in the British Museum, one of the very rarest of men, a librarian who thoroughly knew his business, at all events so far as printed books were concerned, and quite unequalled as regards all questions of organisation and administration. He carries impartiality almost to excess, for he says, speaking of lending, 'It would, perhaps, be expedient to examine the subject more closely before a final determination was come to on either side; for while the Bodleian Library is strictly non-circulating, the books are freely lent out to the members of the University from the University Library of Cambridge, and yet any material difference in the condition of the two libraries to the disadvantage of that of Cambridge, is certainly not a matter of public notoriety.' This statement appeared in 1867, and Mr. Watts evidently did not know that lending had been practised by the Bodleian Curators ever since 1862 (see above, p. 14); nor was he seemingly aware of the facts detailed by Mr. Bradshaw, or of such gross abuses as that which Mr. Bradshaw told a friend of my own. He said that on a certain occasion a graduate had a dinner party, and that he borrowed from the University Library certain expensive illustrated works to be laid on the table to amuse his guests; Bradshaw was powerless, though indignant at an act so disgraceful. Carefully however as Mr. Watts holds the balance, it seems unquestionable that he himself condemned the practice of lending from such libraries as the British Museum or the Bodleian; for after writing a column or more, in which he shows every disposition to lend books where it is possible to do so without causing more harm than good, he considers Mr. Spedding's proposal to lend a book wanted by a reader in London to the British Museum library—the very thing in fact which we now are in the habit of doing, he then says; "By this ingenious arrangement some of the advantages proposed by the lending system would certainly be afforded, under safeguards not now obtainable; but there would still remain the strong objection that a reader wishing to examine a particular book known to be in a particular library might be subjected to a disappointment which he is now in no hazard of. This objection is tersely stated in a passage from a letter by Niebuhr, which was quoted by the Commissioners for examining into the University of Oxford. 'It is lamentable,' writes Niebuhr from the University of Bonn, 'that I am here much worse off for books than I was at Rome, where I was sure to find whatever was in the library, because no books were lent out; here I find that just the book which I most want is always lent out.' There are few libraries from which books are lent of which stories are not current respecting the abuse of the privilege, of volumes kept for years by persons too high or too venerable to be questioned. The rules of such institutions are often laxly observed by those from whom we should least expect such disregard. In Walter Scott's correspondence with Southey there is a passage in which he recommends him not to show publicly a book which he had sent him, because it belongs to the Advocate's Library, and it is forbidden for those books to be sent out of Scotland."

The opinion then of one of the most accomplished librarians that ever lived is, on the whole, adverse to the system of lending. I believe it to be quite impossible for a man of his enormous knowledge of the subject to come to any other conclusion than that at which he arrived: the less a man knows about books and libraries, the more inclined he is to the pernicious system of lending; the more he knows about them, the less inclined he is to countenance anything of the kind; such at least has been my experience.

The late Mr. Henry Bradshaw of Cambridge was a most learned librarian and an accomplished bibliographer. He has not, so far as I am aware, expressed in print his plain opinion of the lending system; but no one can read his paper on the Cambridge University Library, (The University Library, ... by Henry Bradshaw, Librarian of the University, Camb. 1881. 8vo.,) without seeing that he bitterly regretted the practice which prevails and has long prevailed in that place. The Bodleian has a history, a noble and honourable history: the Cambridge University Library has none, at all events none that is not disgraceful. 'One reason,' he says (p. 6), 'for the dearth of materials in the Library for its own history is to be found in the circumstance that the Library is really scattered over the whole country.' And again, 'We have often heard of the principal benefactors to the Bodleian Library having been induced to bequeath their own libraries to the University of Oxford from seeing the careful way in which the bequests of their predecessors have been housed and kept together. The coincidence at Cambridge is too striking to be accidental, where we find that only two such bequests are on record': this statement he subsequently corrects into 'three' instead of two: and again, 'It is probable that by drawing attention to the fact that none of the great collectors of the last two hundred years have thought fit to leave their books to our University Library, we may be pointing to a lesson which our successors may profit by, even though we are too indifferent to pay any attention to it ourselves.'

The inference plainly to be drawn from these and other passages is that the writer strongly disapproved of the practice which he was obliged officially to countenance. From 1600 down to the last ten or fifteen years the history of the Bodleian Library has been on the whole a history of which every true scholar, and every genuine lover of books may be proud; the history of the Cambridge Library for the corresponding period has been an almost unbroken record of disgraceful carelessness, and the root of all the evil has been the practice of lending, as will be clear to any one who will take the trouble to read Mr. Bradshaw's paper. There has been, as there always must be, where such a practice is allowed, wholesale robbery. In 1772 the library was inspected and 'a large number of rare books were reported to be missing.' (p. 28.) The latest previous inspection had been in 1748, when 902 volumes were reported as missing from the old library alone ... the loss was the result of that wholesale pillage spoken of before. It is very singular that the very same year that the inspection shewed such serious losses to have happened from unrestricted access, the University should have made fresh orders (the basis of those now in use), permitting more fully this same freedom of access. The Cicero de Officiis printed in 1465 on vellum, a Salisbury Breviary printed in 1483 on vellum (the only known copy of the first edition), the Salisbury Directorium Sacerdotum printed by Caxton (the only known copy), are three instances out of many scores of such books which might be mentioned as purloined during the latter half of the eighteenth century, simply from this total disregard of all care for the preservation of the books. Even manuscripts were lent out on ordinary tickets; and it was seemingly only owing to the strong remonstrances of Mr. Kerrich, the principal Librarian of the day, that a grace was passed in 1809, requiring that no manuscript whatever should be borrowed, except with the permission of the Senate, and on a bond given for the same to the Librarian. "We have the ticket, but we cannot get the book back," Mr. Kerrich says: "and to this day the book in question has never been returned." (p. 28.) Such are the disgraceful acts of men bred at an English University, compared with whom the common pickpocket appears positively respectable.

Mr. Panizzi, principal Librarian of the British Museum, a man whose knowledge of libraries and of books has rarely been equalled, was asked, 'Are you of opinion that there should be in all countries libraries of two sorts, namely, libraries of deposit, and libraries devoted to general reading and the circulation of books?' answered, 'That is another question. I think the question of lending books is a very difficult question to answer. I have enquired in all countries, and, as far as experience goes, I find that, in spite of all the precautions taken, of the regulations, and of everything which is done, books disappear; they are stolen or spoiled.' (2. R. 62.) And again: 'I do not think that lending can well be adopted without great risk of losing books; the question is whether there might not be remedies; I think from all experience I never found that librarians had succeeded in preventing stealing.' He also tells a very instructive story of some rare books stolen from the library at Wolfenbüttel, and be it noted that Panizzi and Watts knew more of their profession than a whole army of ordinary librarians. Let no one fancy for one moment that a congress of librarians is necessarily a congress of men really acquainted with either bibliography or with books; it may, perhaps, on some occasions include one or more who answer to that description, but in general it does not do so. 'La bibliographie,' says Richou, 'est une science exacte qui demande une préparation assez longue et que la pratique développe. Les bibliothécaires improvisés en ignorent jusqu'à l'existence et se préoccupent peu de l'acquérir. Il ne faut pas chercher ailleurs la cause de la mauvaise administration d'un grand nombre de bibliothèques publiques, car le mal est commun.' (Traité de l'Administration des Bibliothèques publiques, p. 82.)

The opinion expressed by Mr. Watts and Mr. Panizzi, and implied by Mr. Bradshaw, is, I am convinced, the opinion of all men who are acquainted with this question in its length, breadth, and depth.

How comes it then, some one may ask, that foreign librarians do not speak out against the practice? Because it is not in general the habit of foreign officials to have opinions of their own, and still less to express them, if they have them, when such opinions are not fashionable, or not likely to advance those who utter them: and this goes a long way towards explaining the answers given to questions put by the English Government nearly forty years ago to the custodians of libraries where (though under many restrictions) lending was, and is practised. The general tenor of the answers is that books do not suffer more than might be expected, that losses are comparatively rare, that when loss is suffered the books can generally be replaced, and that when they cannot their value can almost always be recovered from the borrower. Such, I say, is the general tenor of the answers, but few who know anything about circulating libraries will accept such answers as satisfactory. Before the outbreak of the Thirty Years' War the Germans printed splendid books, and not unfrequently bound them grandly; but for the last two hundred years few German librarians, unless trained in France or England, have known what a really fine book is, or whether it is in what a Frenchman would call good condition. In other words, when they say that books lent are not much damaged, it must be always remembered that notions of damage are relative, and most German librarians are in all probability like an old friend of my own, who holds that no book is in really ill condition, provided the readable part of it is still legible: the title may be torn or gone; 'I don't want to read the title,' says he: the covers may be broken or destroyed; 'Cannot you read an unbound book?' he asks; and so on. There is this difference, however; my friend does know when a book really is in good condition. Moreover, there are, or at least there were, some foreign librarians who have dared to tell the truth. Thus (see 2. R. 161-171), from the returns made by eighteen libraries in Belgium, we learn that the library of Antwerp (19,148 vols.) never lent; that no manuscripts were ever lent from that of Bruges; that manuscripts and rare books were never lent from the library of Malines; that valuable books were never lent from the library of Louvain; that no manuscripts or valuable books were ever lent from the library of Mons; and that such books and manuscripts were never lent from any of the University libraries. Nevertheless, some lending there was from some libraries; and it was asserted that little damage was done the books. Very different is the answer of the Librarian of Tournay (2. R. 163): 'Cette coutume a des inconvénients assez graves: impossibilité pour certains lecteurs de consulter les ouvrages dont ils ont besoin: rentré tardive des livres prêtés; perte ou détérioration des volumes.' The Librarian of Nassau (2. R. 299), very unlike most of his brethren, says, 'das Verleihen der Bücher asserhalb der Anstalt hat allerdings die nachtheilige Folge dass dieselben in kurzer Zeit, im Aussern wie im Innern stark mitgenommen werden. Die Einbände werden verstossen und schäbig und der Druck durch Schnupfer und Raucher oft aufs Unangenehmste beschmutzt,' with more to the same effect. Even at the Royal Library of Berlin it is admitted that 'die Bücher und Einbände werden dadurch mehr beschädight und verdorben' (2. R. 304); and at the University Library, 'die Abnutzung durch die Studirenden ist sehr stark' (2. R. 305). The answer from the University Library at Bonn is, 'Nachtheilige Folge beim Verleihen der Bücher waren troz der sorgfältigsten Ueberwachung nicht immer zu vermeiden. Manche Bände kamen beschmutzt auch verstümmelt zurück.' There are very similar answers from a few other libraries both of Germany and Italy. Common sense and a little experience will tell any one to which class of testimony credence should be given.

As to replacing a lost or damaged book, the thing is by no means so easy as it looks. What is common to-day may be rare a year hence, and quite unprocurable on any terms in two years time. 'Then,' says Ignoramus, 'it will be reprinted, and you may buy that'; but the man who talks so wildly cannot be argued with, because he does not know the elements of the subject of which he is speaking. Suppose you lose the 19th edition of the Christian Year, you do not replace the book by purchasing the 100th edition, as all experts know. 'Buy another copy of the 19th then', says Ignoramus; but it may be that you have to pay a very high price for it, and it sometimes happens that you cannot get it at all. 'If you do not get the book, you can recover its value.' Even supposing that you can—and here in Oxford we have no machinery by which we can recover a farthing—how is a man who wants to see a particular book benefited by being told that he cannot see the book because it has been lent and lost, but that the Library has received compensation? Well might Panizzi say that the question of lending is a very difficult question; it is so difficult that a volume would hardly contain an enumeration of all its complexities.

Consider the case of books, printed and manuscript, lent out to those on the borrowers' list, a list, be it observed, which, according to the lawyers, has not the least statutable warrant. In the first place, you have not the least assurance or guarantee that any one of them knows how to use a book without damaging it, and, as I have already said, it is an almost uniform and invariable experience, that borrowers of books do damage them. All book-lovers know this so well, that they make very sure of their man before they intrust a valuable or well-bound book to him, but we at the Bodleian do

not. Pixerécourt, a great collector, was so convinced of this fact that he inscribed over his library door these sadly true lines—
Tel est le triste sort de tout livre prêté
Souvent il est perdu, toujours il est gâté.
How unfit some at least on the borrowers' list are to be intrusted with books, how little notion they have of taking care of them, is clear from many facts which might be mentioned. In the library itself you may see almost any day abundant proof of the unfitness of those admitted to enjoy the privileges which are allowed them. On May 19th, 1885, a Curator came into my room and said, 'I was walking through the Bodleian looking for — — when I saw a sight which made me sick.' 'You may see many such sights there,' said I; 'what was it?' 'I saw a bevy of women with an illuminated MS., and they were turning over the leaves, all looking at it.' On Friday, August 21st, 1885, I myself counted at one desk at the Selden end sixty-four volumes, all had out by one reader; on the table was a MS. open, and on it two or three books; another was open on the floor, and so on. On April 22nd, 1886, I saw on a desk also at the Selden end three (I believe four) Sanscrit MSS. They were open and kept so by books placed on them, sundry printed books also open one on the other, and in my note written the same day I find the observation that it was 'a miserable spectacle of untidiness and reckless disregard for precious volumes.' It would be easy to add more, for from the first I have kept notes of all that I see in the library, and of much that I hear about it—this, however, is enough to show what may be expected when people carry off books home. There no prying eye will see them, no one is likely to come suddenly round a corner and observe their proceedings. Things are really bad enough in the library as it is; and they are as bad or worse in the Camera, where books are most shamefully ill-used. I have notes of some things which I have observed there, and of a conversation which I had with a person of sharp eyes and wits. One Curator alone can do very little; if all would, even it were only occasionally, do what I do habitually (Tit. XX. iii. § 12, 2), it would be far easier than it now is to put a stop to some rather serious abuses. Let it be distinctly understood that in saying all this I do not blame any person or persons whatever, except the readers. In the British Museum Reading-room a man placed where the officials sit could, with a machine-gun, comfortably pick off every reader in less than a minute, because he could rake every desk; the Bodleian is so picturesque and so peculiar in its construction, that Argus himself would be completely non-plussed, if ordered to keep his eyes on the readers, for even this highly-endowed being had not the dragon-fly power of seeing round corners; and from the Librarian's seat you might discharge a Gatling gun straight up 'Duke Humphrey,' with no other result than the downfall of a little dust, and the smashing of the west window; as to hitting a reader, you might as well try to shoot the Invisible Girl. At the Camera

there is just the same difficulty, which will hardly be overcome till the laws of nature are reformed, and light condescends to travel in convenient curves. The regular officials have quite enough to do, if they attend only to their necessary work, which pins them down to one spot, and totally precludes them from exercising (even if they possessed it) the saintly privilege of bilocation. To come back to the point: books are badly used in the library itself. Now I ask any man of common sense, whether it is possible that books treated so vilely in the library itself will be better treated in a private house?

I am not going to tell any tales, but this I may say, that before I became a Curator I have seen Bodleian books (once a very rare book) in strange places, and under circumstances by no means conducive to their preservation. The thing must be so: it is as much as the most vigilant officer can do to prevent damage being done under his very eyes, and it stands to reason that no mercy will be shown a book as soon as it is fairly out of the building.

Again, when a man borrows a book from the Bodleian, you have not the least assurance that he will not in his turn lend it. This I know has happened with one book at least belonging to another library in Oxford. Sir Walter Scott had, perhaps, as much conscience as it is possible for a literary man to have, yet he lends Southey a book borrowed from the Advocates' Library (see above, p. 49) contrary to rule; and what Scott would do, Scott's inferior in character and morals would most certainly not scruple to do.

When a book is lent out to any one on the borrowers' list no contract is entered into, either verbally or in writing, that the book shall be returned at any specified time, nor in fact that it shall ever be returned at all. Are the Curators quite sure that they have any legal power to compel a return under such circumstances?

Unless a book is carefully collated when it is returned, it will always be impossible to say with truth that it has been returned intact; and if every book is to be collated on its restoration to the library, we shall have no small increase of work, and increase of work always means, as we well know, increased expense.

The lending of books to private houses then involves the very probable, and in many cases the absolutely certain, damage of the book, and its possible total loss without the least remedy, and without the slightest recompense or penalty. A manuscript was lent to the late Professor , and it is hardly necessary to say that it has never been returned, and this is, I fancy, at least the second instance within a very few years of total loss, for which neither the public nor the University ever received one atom of benefit.

Even if the Bodleian were not one of the two great reference libraries of this country, if it were merely a large and fine library of no very great national importance, there would still be no excuse for borrowing from it;

for there is no town of its size that contains so many books as Oxford. In every College there is a library, which is not unfrequently full of fine books—Christ Church, All Souls', St. John's, Worcester, Merton, Corpus, Oriel, Magdalen and Queen's are all remarkable; and if we count in manuscripts there is hardly a single College without its gems and rarities. Nor is there the slightest difficulty in making a proper use of all these treasures. Any one really fit to use a College book is always permitted to do so, nor is there in general any objection to lending if the borrower is known to be trustworthy: the fault, if any, is rather the other way. 'But,' says some borrower, 'the book that I want is in no College library, and it is in the Bodleian.' Is it not plain to every man of sense, that the book which is in no College library, and is in the Bodleian, is just the book which ought not to be lent, under any conceivable circumstances? Lending even from College libraries has been the cause of innumerable losses—in fact, nothing in Euclid is more true than the proposition, that sooner or later A BOOK LENT IS A BOOK LOST.

Of the losses which the library at Cambridge has sustained, something has been said above (p. 51). All libraries, however carefully kept, are exposed to occasional and exceptional depredations. Paulus, the celebrated German professor, stole one manuscript at least from the Bodleian; the thefts in German, Russian, Italian, and French libraries are only too notorious. Are we to give additional facilities by lending books out? Even when lent to the greatest scholars, and presumably to careful men, books are by no means safe. Every one knows how, not so long ago, two or more of the most ancient manuscripts of Jornandes were destroyed while in the hands of Mommsen. Fire invaded his rooms; the professor escaped unharmed (of course he did), but the manuscripts were destroyed. Literature and scholarship gained nothing by this loan, though all future generations have lost much. Had common sense been the ruling principle of the libraries from which Mommsen obtained these manuscripts, they would have been safe at this moment. The convenience, perhaps the laziness, of an individual was consulted, and the world has lost what can never be replaced.

Mr. Watts, whom I have already quoted, says in speaking of lending, 'The testimony of Molbech, the librarian of the Royal Library of Copenhagen, where lending is permitted, is to the effect, not only that the risk is greater, as must of course be the case where books are removed from supervision and control, but that in practice great damage is found to ensue.' If we are told, as very likely we shall be told, that no such damage occurs here, I am somewhat at a loss to answer; perhaps it will be enough to observe that different men unavoidably have different ideas of what constitutes damage, and that what is not always immediately discovered may hereafter be detected when it is too late to assign the blame to the real offender.

Under the present system of administration, for which the Curators are responsible, the actual, and, it may be, the unavoidable wear and tear of books in the library itself, even in the choicer portions of it, is great enough to deter any man in the future from acting as Douce did in the past. The way in which very precious volumes are knocked about is plain enough to any one who visits the interior of the library as constantly as I do, and as all Curators are by statute empowered and even ordered to do. Readers are impatient, sometimes unreasonable; immense numbers of books can only be reached by means of ladders; the whole establishment is undermanned, and though the small staff does its best to protect the books, they are notwithstanding much bumped about. One consequence of this rough usage is that the standard of carefulness, as it may be called, is very naturally lowered, and as a further consequence the estimate of what constitutes damage is lowered in proportion.

There are many readers, or there certainly have been readers in the library, who have not hesitated to make marks in printed books and manuscripts. The man who will do such a thing as this in the library, will not hesitate to do it when he gets the book into his own possession. Now all avoidable wear and tear is so much real loss to the library, and detracts in that proportion from its utility. It may be useful to A or B to borrow books from the Bodleian, but it cannot be useful to the University or to future generations that the life of any book should be carelessly or needlessly abridged.

It will be admitted that no book can be in two places at the same time; if a volume is in the rooms of Mr. X or Mr. Y, it cannot at that moment be produced in the Bodleian should a reader happen to want it. One of the great advantages of such a library as the Bodleian, if it were properly administered, is that a visitor is sure to find the book which he comes to consult. This is perfectly well understood by such men as Mr. Watts (see above, p. 49); it was brought home to the mind of Niebuhr, and it has been one of the reasons why all lending has up to the present moment been most rigidly forbidden at the British Museum. In a library like the Bodleian, where the practice of lending prevails as it now does, a man may put himself to great inconvenience in order to visit it; he may even travel from Berlin, and when he arrives he may find that all his trouble has been in vain; the very book he wants is out: at the British Museum, where up to the present time knowledge and common sense have prevailed, every man is sure that he can at once get any book whatever that he finds in the catalogue. It is a thousand pities to destroy this confidence; one of the great uses of a library like ours disappears when things are so ill managed, and I believe that there are in the Bodleian men who could tell of some grievous disappointments caused by our modern laxity. I know very well that we shall be told that such cases are few and trivial: be it so. Who does not see that as the present practice extends, as extend it must, one of the great advantages of a grand library will at last vanish? Nothing can be more strictly useful to all real students than the absolute certainty of obtaining at once any book that can be found in the catalogue.

No limit seems to be placed on the borrower's powers; he may, for anything that appears to the contrary, have any number of books or manuscripts out. Now when we see the practice of more than one reader in the library, we may form a pretty shrewd guess of what men will do in the way of borrowing. I am well within the mark when I say that at least one hundred volumes have been ere now allowed out to one reader at a time.

The present Librarian has been trying, I believe, to check this morbid appetite for superfluous volumes; but it is not always an easy thing to root out a bad habit.

Any one who examines the slips in the various parts of the Bodleian, as I habitually do, will be struck by two things; the immense number of volumes had out by the same reader or readers, and the length of time that volumes are allowed to remain off the shelves; and this is in great measure the fault of a system for which we are answerable. What takes place in the library will undoubtedly sooner or later take place out of it. A borrower is not, so far as I know, limited as to the number of volumes he may have out; neither is he limited as to the time he may keep them out. The present Librarian informed me that when he came into office he found that one book had been out of the library for nine years, and that others had been off the shelves for very long periods of time. And such things must happen, if you sanction this wretched system of lending. It is perfectly easy to do what constant experience has shown to entail on the whole the minimum of evil; it is easy to keep your books within the library as they do at the British Museum; but if you once lend, there is no drawing of lines possible. Altogether there are about one hundred and eleven persons on the borrowers' list already. It is said that the Curators can refuse any application if they choose; of course they can, but as a matter of fact no application ever has been refused, and every name added will make it more and more difficult, more and more invidious to refuse any one. Every Oxford resident is potentially on the list, and he may be actually on it whenever he likes. What is this but the beginning, and something more than the beginning, of that wretched system which Mr. Bradshaw speaks of above? (p. 50.) The dissolution of our magnificent library is already insidiously begun; and why is all this gratuitous and irreparable mischief to be done? why is that vast storehouse intended for the use and benefit of generation after generation of scholars to be scattered and at last destroyed? Simply to gratify the vulgar, selfish convenience of this or that individual regardless of the general good. The whole is to be sacrificed for a part, and for what a part! The present Librarian has been trying to do something to check this disastrous and ruinous practice, but the Curators are responsible for it, not the Librarian.

Manuscripts and printed books when lent out of Oxford are as a rule not lent to private houses but deposited in some library. What happens abroad I do not know, though I confess to having my suspicions. If a manuscript were lent to some one in a Cathedral town, it would be deposited in the Cathedral library; and we comfort ourselves with the belief that in such a place it would be secure, and that it would not on any account be removed from that library elsewhere. An acquaintance of my own, a very safe man, has had a Bodleian manuscript of great value out for some years, and it is lent not to him directly, but to a library where alone he is to use it. It may be that this arrangement is actually carried out, and I do not know that it is not, yet I would bet five pounds to a penny that if I went to his house I should find the Bodleian book kicking about in his study, where, in fact, though exposed to a thousand risks of damage and even destruction, it is really safer than in the library where we suppose it to be. For one Cathedral library I can answer: a book would hardly be safer there than it would be on a public and unwatched book-stall, and such I have no doubt whatever is the case with more than half the places to which we send books for safe custody. There is as little conscience about books in this stupid and wicked world as there is about umbrellas, and one of the most important and most useful functions of a body like the Curators of the Bodleian is to set up a high standard in such matters. It is our duty as trustees to take lofty ground, and to be sensitive where the world is listless and careless; and even if we do not really feel exactly as we ought, we are bound, like Gertrude, to 'assume a virtue though we have it not'; it is very laudable hypocrisy if the real article cannot be had. Yet I hope that it can, and that upon consideration we may all see that the convenience of a few is not for a moment to be compared with the convenience of many, and that we shall awake to the fact that we, of all people, ought not to countenance in any way whatever any practice which may tend in the remotest degree to damage the only institution in Oxford of which any rational being can in the present day be justly proud.

Lending of books has many more evil consequences, proximate and remote, than I have enumerated; but there is one which at the risk of being tedious must be mentioned. The glorious part of the Bodleian, the part contributed by Bodley himself, by Laud, by Selden, Pembroke, Digby, Roe, Rawlinson, andc., consists largely of gifts. Every man who knows anything at all about books, every one who loves them, is perfectly well aware that very few men will bequeath their libraries to an institution which emulates the American or the English circulating and commercial establishment. Barlow knew this, Bradshaw knew it (see above, p. 50); every one knows it, who has the least acquaintance with the habits and peculiarities of collectors. The Bodleian has to my certain knowledge already lost very rare books indeed which it might have had, but for this penny-wise and pound-foolish policy. Neither Rawlinson nor Douce would ever have been such fools as to leave us what they did, could they have foreseen how little sense of our duties and of our interests we have shown. Bodley over and over again, and in the strongest terms, forbad the lending of his books; Selden's executors only delivered his books to us on the express condition that they never should under any circumstances be lent; Laud stipulated that his books should not be lent, except for one particular purpose and in one particular way. The Bodleian is what it is, because till quite recent times we adhered to the rule of common sense, not to say to that of common honesty, and it is ever to be regretted that we departed from a course which was at once safe and honourable. There will be no more Douces, no more Rawlinsons, until we have returned to better ways and proved the sincerity of our repentance. I have heard it maintained that the days of great benefactors are over, that in some way not explained men's characters and habits have changed. I cannot admit this; men are now what they always were, and collectors in all ages are singularly alike. Only let us be as prudent, as worldly wise, and, I will add, as honest as our predecessors were, and there is no reason why the munificent benefactors of the past should not be rivalled by equally munificent benefactors in the future. Mr. Bradshaw (above, p. 50) is decidedly of opinion that carelessness with regard to books prevents benefactions, and that care attracts them. Barlow is of the same mind, and indeed the thing is too obvious to be insisted on. It is only those who know little or nothing of the feelings which actuate the real lovers of books who doubt about such very simple facts as these.

To conclude this part of the subject; the arguments against the lending of books out of such a library as the Bodleian may be briefly summed up thus: lending is bad, because books are necessarily exposed to needless and certain risks of damage and of downright loss; because one of the great ends served by a large library is defeated, in that no man can be certain of obtaining a book known to be in it; because lending leads sooner or later to the destruction of a library; because it dries up the great sources from which large numbers of the most valuable books are derived; because it is disapproved of by all those who have the largest and widest experience of books and their management; because, finally, it is in violation of the express directions of Bodley, of Selden, of Laud and others, and almost certainly contrary to the wishes of all our great benefactors, even though they may not have said as much. Reason and authority are equally against it; and the cause of learning and of literature can never be permanently served by a practice which tends to destroy that without which learning and literature alike are impossible: whatever advantages may seem to attend it, are more than counterbalanced by disadvantages so great, that none but those who recklessly sacrifice the future to the present, the interests of generations yet to come, to the selfishness of the generation that now is, can regard it with any favour or even with common patience. We have by the sturdy honesty of our predecessors received a vast treasure which they carefully preserved intact; we are its guardians and trustees, and we are bound in honour and honesty to hand on to our successors, undiminished and unimpaired, what we have received only as a trust, not as a something which we may spend or destroy at our pleasure. Any wilful act of ours which tends, however remotely, to damage the Bodleian Library is not only a scandalous breach of duty, but a crime against learning itself, in which I for one will have no part or share.